Wings like a Dove

CHOSEN DAUGHTERS

Wings like a Dove

The Courage of Queen Jeanne d'Albret

Christine Farenhorst

P&R

PUBLISHING

P.O. BOX 817 • PHILLIPSBURG • NEW JERSEY 08865-0817

Scripture quotations are from The Holy Bible, English Standard Version, copyright © 2001 by Crossway Bibles, a division of Good News Publishers. Used by permission. All rights reserved.

Page design by Dawn Premako

Typesetting by Lakeside Design Plus

Printed in the United States of America

Library of Congress Cataloging-in-Publication Data

Farenhorst, Christine, 1948–
    Wings like a dove : the courage of Queen Jeanne d'Albret / Christine Farenhorst.
        p. cm.—(Chosen daughters)
    Includes bibliographical references (p.).
    Summary: In the mid-sixteenth century, as Jeanne grows from a mischievous child to the queen of Navarre, she increasingly supports the Huguenots, who would reform the Catholic faith despite persecution by her cousin, the king of France, and other European rulers.
        ISBN-13: 978-0-87552-642-3 (pbk.)
        ISBN-10: 0-87552-642-X (pbk.)
        1. Jeanne d'Albret, Queen of Navarre, 1528–1572—Juvenile fiction. [1. Jeanne d'Albret, Queen of Navarre, 1528–1572—Fiction. 2. Reformation—Fiction. 3. Huguenots—Fiction. 4. Basques—Fiction. 5. Navarre (Kingdom)—Fiction. 6. France—History—16th century—Fiction.] I. Title II. Series.

PZ7.F22297Win 2006
[Fic]—dc22
                                        2005053909

Dedicated to

Emma Christine, Stephanie Elizabeth, Keturah Kristin,
Zoë Hadassah, Havilah Abigail, Keziah Grace, Tirzah
Gail, Beatrice Sandra, and Noelle Beatrix,
all of them little princesses in their own homes
by virtue of Him who loved them
and washed them from their sins in His own blood.
To Him be glory and dominion forever and ever.

CONTENTS

ACKNOWLEDGMENTS

A heartfelt thank you to Emberlee, Elineke, Charity, and Karina, who proofread pages and were totally encouraging. As well, a hug for Claire Bedard who read the entire manuscript twice, correcting and advising on the French that was used. Thanks also to Karen Teeter for her valiant efforts in helping to locate the hard-to-find inter-library loan books. And last of all, a bouquet of patience to Ranelda Hunsicker who made wise suggestions throughout and added her expertise on a number of occasions.

My heart is in anguish within me;

the terrors of death have fallen upon me.

Fear and trembling come upon me,

and horror overwhelms me.

And I say, "Oh, that I had wings like a dove!

I would fly away and be at rest;

yes, I would wander far away;

I would lodge in the wilderness;

I would hurry to find a shelter

from the raging wind and tempest."

Psalm 55:4—8

I

LONRAY

The little girl wore a blue satin dress, her small skirt open at the front displaying a pretty kirtle with a lark embroidered on it. The hanging sleeves on her arms trailed the floor as she sat on her knees playing with some toys. Gold and silver, these toys lay strewn about in front of the hearth. The child hummed a song to herself as she moved about miniature lamps, chairs, and tables. A tiny chamber pot the size of her fingernail was carefully tucked away under a small-scale canopied bed. The hearth fire glowed and crackled and a great black dog lay nearby, red tongue lolling out of her mouth as she watched her mistress amuse herself. At length Jeanne, for that was the child's name, grew tired of her "le petit ménage," her little household, and yawned. She was bored.

A tapestry lay draped over the table. Its warm colors invited touch, and, for lack of anything else to do, Jeanne ambled over to it. The design on the tapestry depicted a monk eating at a table. Lifting a blue satin arm, she let her fingers delight in the softness of the embroidery. She had watched her governess, Aymée, work her needle at this piece destined to be a wall hanging. Not large, it would do well as a covering for Noir, her dog. Fleetingly she considered that Aymée would not like a holy monk to cover a dog. But Aymée was taking a nap in her room and not here. Jeanne ran her thumb over the monk's face, sliding the embroidery across the table a bit and a scissors fell to the floor.

Without thinking, she picked them up and continued her study of the monk. He was fat, this monk, and looked crafty. Monsieur Bourbon, her teacher, often said that monks were crafty, as crafty as foxes. There was a picture of a fox in one of the books over by the shelf in the corner. Wouldn't the monk look terribly funny with the face of a fox! Before she knew it, her feet had carried her over to the shelf and her hands had opened the book to the right page. The fox grinned at her and she grinned back. The scissors snipped and she carried Reynard back to the table. It was a little more difficult cutting through the tapestry but at length a beautiful and gaping hole showed where the monk's face had been. She fitted the fox picture in, securing it between loose threads. She admired the new hooded animal face greatly until suddenly the immensity of what she had done struck her. What would Aymée say? Dragging the wall hanging over to a corner, she hid it in a chest.

"Your sins shall find you out."

It was as if Monsieur Bourbon whispered the words into her ear, and she looked over her shoulder, fearful lest he had sneaked into the room without her hearing him. But he was not there, and she breathed a sigh of relief, remembering that he had left for England more than a week ago and that she was doing all her lessons with Aymée right now.

Dinnertime came without Aymée discovering the damage done to her tapestry. Believing her small charge to have been very good all afternoon, she brought Jeanne's food on a special plate from which she was sometimes allowed to eat if she had been particularly well behaved. The plate was Aymée's treasured possession because her husband François, now long dead, had given it to her. In raised silver it pictured David killing a lion. Jeanne, although nagged by a slight feeling of guilt, quickly drowned it in her feeling of delight. When her food was gone, her index finger traced the outline of David's arm and his tunic. Feeling brave, she also gingerly touched the lion's tawny mane as well as his sharp claws. Aymée noticed the little girl's trepidation and teased her.

"It's not real, Jeanne. The lion can't scratch or bite you. It's only a plate."

Jeanne quickly dropped her hand into her lap and angrily tightened her round lips. She did not at all like the suggestion that she might be frightened.

"I think that maybe David was a little afraid. Just a little."

Aymée smiled at her and Jeanne, slightly mollified, went on.

"Anyway, how could David kill a lion? What made him so strong?"

"God helped him," Aymée answered.

Jeanne was five years old. "Almost six" had been her middle name for a great part of the year. She was a princess. Her father and mother were the king and queen of Navarre and her uncle was the king of France. But if someone had asked her whom she herself would choose as father or mother, were such a thing possible, she would have said André the baker and Toinette the wet nurse. André was the jolliest man imaginable, always laughing and always ready to slip her a sweetmeat. And

Toinette—well, Toinette loved her and thought everything Jeanne did was wonderful.

"To be a princess," Aymée told her again and again, "is your station in life. You are different and that is why you must learn to speak properly, to walk properly, and to act as befits a royal person."

"But I have five fingers on each hand," Jeanne rejoined.

"What has that to do with anything?"

"Well," Jeanne said thoughtfully, "Toinette has five fingers on each of her hands. Yvette does too and so does Monsieur Perault, the stable master. So I am like them and not different."

"No," Aymée answered rather sharply, "you are not like them. You are an Albret. You have royal blood."

"But my blood is red just like Toinette's," Jeanne giggled. "I know it is because when she cut herself last week, I saw it and when I pricked myself on a thorn—"

"Hush, Jeanne, hush!"

Aymée was to be obeyed. This was a fact, and although Jeanne did not always do so, she had learned very early on in life that when she did obey, things were much easier. Her father and mother, in the kingdom of Navarre, were as far away from Jeanne as the sun was away from the moon. Lonray, an estate in Normandy, France, was Aymée's home and that was where Jeanne lived.

On the whole, Lonray was a pleasant place to live. It was an estate far more elegant than many of the neighboring old Norman houses, and Jeanne was quite pleased to live there. Aymée's husband, François, had tried to make it very attractive when he had married his beautiful bride.

"A lovely house for a lovely wife," he had said. Masons had been hired to construct wonderful stone columns and sculptures on the grounds. Gardeners had also been hired to design a large park around the house with a high wall to close it off from outsiders. The park had wide lanes, large trees, sparkling fountains, and exotic flowerbeds. Weather permitting, Aymée and Jeanne often went for a walk in the park each morning. The thickly wooded forest of Ecouves lay to the northwest of Lonray and deer often wandered from these woods into the park.

The morning after she had cut a hole into the tapestry Jeanne ran off to the stables to beg some grain from Monsieur Perault, in the hope of feeding some deer. Monsieur Perault, who was very fond of the little princess, readily gave her a handful. She ran back outside to Aymée, who scolded her for bothering the stable master. Jeanne's head hung down, and she hid the grain inside her cape. But as they walked the grounds, her dejection quickly turned to joy because she spotted a few deer alongside the first knoll. Racing ahead of Aymée, she reached the hillock, still clasping her fistful of grain. Standing perfectly still, she stretched out her right hand and hoped that one of the deer would be tempted to come and feed. After what seemed like an eternity, one of them did approach her and began to nibble at the grain on her cupped palm. Half-bold and half-fearful, she could feel the animal's tongue warm and wet on her skin, and her free left hand carefully stole up to stroke its glossy fur. It did not move away.

"My name is Jeanne d'Albret, Monsieur Daim," she whispered. "I was born November 16, 1528, and it will be my birthday soon."

The deer's nearness and its big, solemn eyes filled her with a deep sense of gladness.

"Do you ever see your maman or papa?" she continued softly, casting a quick glance over her shoulder at Aymée who was bent over, gathering some late acorns under a large oak.

"I never do see mine, except sometimes," Jeanne confided. "They are very busy ruling Navarre, you see. Besides that, Maman often goes to the Paris court to see King François. He is my uncle, and needs her help to rule all of France because France is so very big."

The deer nibbled on, his eyes never leaving her face.

"And, Monsieur Daim, if you eat grain all the time, why isn't your skin grain-colored? I must drink milk because Aymée says it will make my skin white, but I do not think that I believe her. Why, my teacher Monsieur Bourbon drinks the wine of the grapes all the time during his lessons with me and his skin is not purple. But," and she stopped to smile engagingly at the deer, "it is true that his nose is a little purple."

The last bit of grain disappeared into the deer's mouth. After one final grating lick on the palm of her small hand, the deer turned and strolled away. Jeanne walked behind him for a few steps. She hated to see him go. He stopped by an oak and rubbed his velvet antlers against its trunk.

"I like your crown," she said, "and someday I will have one too. Just like Papa and Maman. That is what Monsieur Bourbon says."

It was no use. The deer would not come back to her. Picking up a broken branch, she held it behind her right ear. And just when she had spotted a second branch that would do very well for her left ear, Aymée called.

"Jeanne. It's time to go in. We must not be late in studying the lessons Monsieur Bourbon prepared."

The child sighed. There were always the lessons. She briefly tried to put them off.

"Can I look for some acorns too, like you were doing? I might find some big enough for my dolls to use as tea cups."

Aymée simply shook her head.

Later that morning heavy snow began to fall. Flakes twirled about the windows, and Aymée said that winter was now on its way. She moved her chair closer to the hearth and commanded Jeanne to recite the provinces of France.

"Lyonnais, Languedoc, Provence . . ."

Jeanne's voice faltered but not for long. She continued.

"Dauphine, Guyenne . . ."

She stopped.

"Is Papa the governor of Guyenne, Aymée?"

Aymée, from her place at the hearth, nodded languidly. The warmth of the fire had made her rather sleepy.

"You know he is, Jeanne."

The wind gusted eerily, fluting through the eaves. It reminded Jeanne of the *tchirula*, a three-holed pipe, that the Basque musicians in Papa's Navarre played. She smiled, stood up, and began to dance and to chant in a singsong voice.

"My papa, my papa, is govern . . ."

She did not finish because Aymée sat up in her chair and stopped her rather wearily.

"The provinces, Jeanne. Recite the provinces."

Jeanne sighed.

". . . Burgundy, Champagne, Ile-de-France, Picardy, and Normandy."

She stopped, pretending to be finished. Aymée smiled and praised her.

"Bon! That's good, Jeanne. Very good, indeed. You got them all."

"No, I didn't," Jeanne chortled gleefully because she had fooled her governess, "I missed Brittany."

Now it was Aymée's turn to sigh. "Take out your Latin notebook, Jeanne."

"Can a person sigh in Latin, Aymée?"

Aymée considered whether the princess was being rude or creative, but before she could quite make up her mind Yvette came in, curtsying as she spoke.

"It is time for the noon meal, Madame de Lafayette."

2

FATHER LARAT

Jeanne did not have any friends her own age. There was only Yvette, a serving girl, who had been designated by Aymée as *mère de la folle de Madame la princesse*, someone with whom to play. But she was ten years older than Jeanne and had other chores as well. As such, she was not a real, bosom friend, the kind that Jeanne desired. Sometimes Aymée's grandson Jacques visited, but he was three years younger than the princess and still slept in a cradle.

Jeanne, who longed for coziness, often crept into the kitchen when she was not at lessons. It was the warmest and most completely furnished room at Lonray. Benches, stools, tables and chests, and many utensils cluttered around in haphazard fashion. Bacon, ham, and herbs hung suspended from the ceiling. Jeanne liked the smell. Against the south wall were several beds for the servants, and two easy chairs stood near the fire for Aymée and Jeanne. Jeanne absorbed the hustle and bustle and talk of the household like a small sponge. When she was in that room, she became part of the fellowship in the kitchen. There was a certain sense of belonging, and she was glad that she and Aymée ate there almost every day. It was only when there was important company, such as her maman or papa, that they ate in the *grande salle*, their formal dining room.

In the early afternoon Aymée, leaving Yvette in charge of Jeanne, retired to her room. The girls played chess. But Yvette yawned so hugely that, as a joke, Jeanne placed a pawn in her mouth. After spluttering in anger, Yvette refused to pay any attention to either her queen or king, eventually falling asleep on top of the cushions in front of the hearth of the *grande salle*, where they were sitting.

Jeanne wandered off across the hall to the kitchen. For a while she was content to feed table scraps to the dogs. She then grew a bit dozy herself and sat down on the floor, resting her head against the back of Noir, her very own dog. Almost under the table, the child and her pet stretched out flat on the freshly laid rushes covering the floor. The kitchen staff was preparing the chief meal of the day, which would be eaten in the late afternoon. Toinette, scrubbing a cast iron pan, had already companionably winked as Jeanne came in, and she had winked back. Eventually, to the noise of the scouring of vessels and the cutting of vegetables, Jeanne fell asleep. She dreamt about her birthday and of all the things Aymée might allow her to do on that day and of presents that her mother and father might send.

She awoke not too much later to the sound of a loud voice. It came from the direction of the hearth.

". . . churches and buildings everywhere were plastered with placards . . . horrible documents slandering the pope."

The rather scratchy voice stopped and then went on, rising in volume.

"The mass, prayers for the dead, transubstantiation—all these good things were mocked. I am surprised you did not hear of it."

Jeanne cautiously raised her head and saw that Father Larat sat in Aymée's chair. Across from him was Nicolas Jouanne, the steward. Father Larat, a priest from Paris, every now and then came to Lonray with a letter from King François, her uncle. She did not like Father Larat, but perhaps Uncle François had sent him here today with a present for her birthday.

"It was not only in Paris that this horrible insult to the holy faith took place. It occurred in every large city of the kingdom."

Monsieur Jouanne fidgeted uncomfortably. He was not a philosophical man. This kind of talk bothered him, especially from a priest he knew to be dishonest.

"Indeed," he responded softly, "we had no such trouble here, nor have I heard of trouble in Alençon . . ."

Father Larat did not let him finish.

"Alençon!"

He fairly spat the name out, and Jeanne pricked up her ears. Alençon, just to the south of Lonray, was a place she frequently visited. Her mother, the queen of Navarre, was also the duchess of Alençon. Father Larat continued.

"Alençon is an evil place. It is no better than the rest of France. I saw a notice posted there with my own eyes as I traveled through on my way up here. It read that unless France repents of the Mass in sackcloth and ashes, she will perish."

"Perish?" Monsieur Jouanne repeated the word rather stupidly and dully.

"Yes, perish. Can you understand the gall of whoever did this?" Father Larat paused, rubbing his fat hands together before he went on. "His Most Royal Majesty, King François, was shocked."

Jeanne stroked the dog. She never listened carefully to what Father Larat spouted. Yvette said that Father Larat's tongue was more active than a broom because he swept up so much dirt with it. She had tried, after that, to look at his tongue. But it seemed to her, as far as she could see, that it was plain and red, just like her own. His teeth were brown stumps though. Perhaps that was because of all the dirt his tongue had swept in.

Her attention wandered as she snuggled back against Noir for comfort. She had only seen Uncle François a few times. He usually chucked her under the chin, asked Aymée about her health, and then ignored her. When Maman visited, she often spoke of him.

"Your Uncle François, Jeanne, is the most important man in France."

She wondered if he wore his crown to bed. If she ever became a queen like Maman, she would never wear a crown to bed, but she might ask for a bowl of sweetmeats before she went to sleep. Surely queens could command such a thing! The grating, unpleasant voice of Father Larat rasped into her musings.

"The king was so angry that he left his palace at Blois and came back to Paris to see who was responsible for these insolences. I can tell you that when heretical papers were found tacked to the gates of the Louvre as well as to the door of his private apartments, he was angry. He does not tolerate anyone defying royal authority."

Jeanne sat up again and peeked at the men by the hearth. Monsieur Jouanne was quiet before Father Larat's flood of words. It did not appear that anyone else was listening to Father Larat. The bakers and the pastry-maker worked on, rolling out their dough on the counters. The other servants banged about with pots and pans. Even though things in the kitchen were loud, Jeanne felt by looking at Father Larat that his anger was even louder. Even from a distance, Jeanne saw beads of angry sweat break out on his face. She guessed that he did not like whoever it was who had written all those papers. Behind her Noir twitched in his sleep. Toinette, who was polishing a copper kettle, winked at Jeanne and made a face. Jeanne made one back.

"Do you know," Father Larat's voice rose somewhat in the din of noise about him, although he glanced around furtively before he continued, "do you know that even the king's sister, Marguerite of Navarre, is not above suspicion?"

Jeanne half stood up, almost banging her head against the table edge.

"What do you mean?"

Monsieur Jouanne was startled into words.

"Many people complain," Father Larat said, "that Queen Marguerite is friendly with the Lutherans and that her chaplain, Roussel, preaches things contrary to our holy mother church."

Jeanne left the warmth and relative security under the table and crept forward, closer to the chairs.

"Have you not heard that she has written a poem for which she was summoned to court? She called it 'Miroir,' and it is full of heresy."

The word heresy struck a familiar chord with Jeanne. Yes, she remembered Maman had used the word once when she had told her a story about a man who had been burned somewhere.

"Do you know what François our royal liege has said? He has said that all who had to do with this business should be seized and that all heresy should be stamped out."

Father Larat stood up and stamped his right foot on the floor to illustrate his words. The black robe he wore fell heavily about his shapeless form, and he groaned in agitation. Jeanne got up as well and walked over. She parked herself in front of the priest, small hands on her hips, the blue satin dress with the pretty kirtle billowing about her. The black dog woke up and lifted his great head out from under the table to see why his petite mistress had left him.

"Do you mean to burn my mother at the . . . at the . . ."

She could not recall the word her mother had used and turned her head to where the staff was making noise at the great oven.

"At the oven?"

She finished grandly, drawing herself up to her full small stature, all the while eyeing Father Larat in an imperious manner. The priest was taken aback. He had not known that the child was in the kitchen. He smiled benignly.

"I am sure that your mother, may the Virgin be gracious to her, knows how to defend herself. You need not worry about it, ma petite Princesse."

"You may not speak badly of my mother in this house. And if you do, you must leave."

Jeanne's voice was demanding, and Aymée, who was just walking into the kitchen, stopped the child immediately.

"Jeanne, Father Larat is a guest here. You must apologize to him."

Jeanne stamped her foot even as the priest had done.

"I will not. He has said something wicked about Maman, she who is queen of Navarre, and he should not do so."

Jeanne almost choked on her words, she was so angry. And, turning to the black robed priest, she fairly spit out, "You are . . . you are a fox."

Monsieur Jouanne hid a smile behind his hand, and the staff rattled pots and pans in applause for the child because no one was fond of the priest. In the end Jeanne was sent to her room without eating the chief meal. It was a punishment both for having insulted the priest and for having cut up the tapestry, which Aymée had just discovered in the chest. Turning back to Father Larat, Aymée apologized for the child's outburst and offered him a drink of mulled cider, a gesture that placated the agitated priest.

3

DUSK

"Why did Father Larat say those things? You know, about Maman and some other people . . . calling them heterics?"

"Heretics," Aymée absently corrected Jeanne.

"Well, why did he say them?"

Jeanne's gray eyes were bright with questions as she swung her feet over the edge of her bed. Yvette stood in the shadows, waiting for a signal from Madame de Lafayette to begin brushing Jeanne's long hair.

"Your Maman," Aymée began, "likes to help people. She especially likes to help people who might worship just a bit differently than the Roman Catholic Church worships."

"To help people is a good thing."

Jeanne said it matter-of-factly and then yawned.

There was a silence after that except for the crackling of the logs on the hearth. Just as Aymée, who very much disliked discussing topics like heretics, hoped the conversation was finished, the child added another question.

"How do these people worship differently?"

"Well," Aymée began and then stopped, pondering her answer. She clasped her hands together as she spoke, and the green sleeves of her dress shimmered in the firelight. She wished Monsieur Bourbon had postponed his visit to England so that he could instruct Jeanne in these matters.

"Well," she repeated slowly, "these people usually do not pray to the image of the Virgin Mary. That is one thing."

There was a stone statue of the Virgin Mary in the Lonray chapel. Jeanne often went to the chapel with Aymée and had been taught to genuflect in front of it. When she bent her knees, Jeanne frequently peeked up at Mary's face. Mary never stared back at her. Her marble eyes simply gazed up blankly at the great gilded ceiling. Sometimes Jeanne followed the gaze but she had never discovered what it was that so entranced the Virgin. After all, there was nothing to see beyond the ribbed vault of the roof.

"Is it wrong to pray to the Virgin Mary?" Jeanne asked in all seriousness, and just as Aymée was carefully formulating a reply, the child began to grin.

"Oh, Aymée, there is a spider on your shoulder. A little spider . . ."

She got no further, because Aymée jumped up with a shriek, wiping her shoulders with exaggerated motions. Jeanne rolled over on the bed shaking with suppressed laughter. Yvette, a broad smile on her face, stepped out of the shadows. She checked Madame de Lafayette's dress carefully and could find nothing. Angrily Aymée scolded the child.

"You didn't really see anything. You were just trying to frighten me."

"No! No!" Jeanne said, still struggling not to laugh. "There was a spider! There was, Aymée! Really!"

Aymée, exasperated, sighed. The incident tweaked her memory, bringing back to mind the ruined tapestry.

"You were a most ill-behaved child today, Jeanne, and caused much grief. I think it is time to brush her hair, Yvette. And please see to it that she goes to bed right after that."

After Aymée had left and Yvette was brushing her hair, Jeanne returned to the matter of praying to the Virgin Mary. Yvette brushed hard and her scalp tingled, so much that it was difficult to speak.

"Do you . . . pray to . . . the Virgin. . . . Mary, Yvette?"

Yvette shrugged and stopped her work for a minute.

"Sometimes, yes, I do. If I am in trouble, or need something, well, then the priest says, 'Light a candle to the Virgin Mary.' And because I want no trouble, well, then I buy a candle and light it for the Virgin Mary."

"Does it help?"

Yvette shrugged again and renewed her vigorous brushing.

"Sometimes—sometimes not. But I know two things."

She lowered her voice dramatically.

"One—that priests like money, and two—that the princess Jeanne has to go to sleep."

It did not matter what Jeanne said after that. Yvette was adamant. She drew the great curtains in front of the window, tucked the princess in, and left the room.

The fire turned to embers in the hearth. Its light smoldered, rosy and warm. Jeanne's day had been so busy and filled with so many things that her thoughts flitted here and there. After a good deal of tossing and turning, she fell asleep. Tapestries, spiders, and the wind howling outside all melded together into a dream.

In her dream Jeanne ran through a vast meadow by a meandering river. Perhaps the river was the Seine, she did not know, but she flew as if she had wings on her feet. It snowed thickly, and as she glided through the air, she caught fat flakes on her tongue. The wind blew and everything around her—the brown trees, the green grass, the flowers, and the rocks—became coated with white. Beginning to shiver in her long, white nightdress, Jeanne's feet now moved slower and slower. Eventually she froze. Her feet turned into blocks of ice. Suddenly Father Larat stood in front of her. His dark eyes stared at Jeanne for a very long time without blinking. Gradually his facial features changed into those of a fox, and he opened his mouth. Brown, stumpy teeth snarled at her. Jeanne screamed—a loud and piercing scream. She clutched the sheets and rolled against the wooden slats of her bed. The next instant Yvette, who slept in a small outer room, had her arms around Jeanne, soothing and crooning.

"It's all right. It's just a bad dream. Shh! Shh!"

Jeanne was wide awake now. Yvette lit some candles, placed them on the clothes chest, and returned to hold the little girl close. In the flickering shadows, both girls saw the door open. Aymée walked in. She had been preparing for bed, and her hair was covered by a lace bed-cap, which fastened under her chin.

"What is the matter?"

Her voice was angry.

Yvette answered while she stroked Jeanne's cheeks.

"She had a bad dream."

Aymée fixed stern eyes on the child.

"I think I know," she said, "why that is. Bad actions always lead to bad dreams."

Jeanne whimpered. Her arms tightened about Yvette and her face was white. Seeing her distress, Aymée softened somewhat, and she also sat down on the edge of the bed.

"All right. All right, my treasure," she said softly. "We will forget all about today and do better tomorrow."

Jeanne reveled in the attention and soaked it up. The warmth of Yvette's sturdy body as well as Aymée's concerned face made her feel much better. Her finger reached out to play with the strings of Aymée's lace cap.

"Can I go sledding tomorrow?" she wheedled.

Slightly vexed at Jeanne's ability to turn a situation to her own advantage, Aymée tried the same strategy.

"Are you sorry, Jeanne, for the things you have done wrong today?"

The child nodded half-heartedly, her head snug on Yvettte's shoulder.

"Are you truly sorry?" Aymée persisted.

Again Jeanne nodded, drowsily lisping an afterthought, "Monsieur Perault has last year's sled in the stable. He showed it to me a few days ago."

She was speaking of the cow's skull the stable master had fashioned into a small sled for the princess the previous winter. Supervised by Yvette, she'd slid down some of the steep embankments and hills around Lonray, shrieking with laughter as she did so.

"Yes, yes, you may go sledding tomorrow. But," Aymée added, "only if you go back to sleep right away."

Jeanne was already oblivious to the world. Yvette eased her back onto the pillow and snuffed out the candles. An owl hooted in the distance.

4

CONFRONTATION

Four months later Jeanne went to visit her parents, the king and queen of Navarre. Their kingdom, in the southernmost corner of France, lay on the nether side of the Pyrenees and held many beautiful valleys, hills, and vineyards. Béarn, Albret, Bigorre, Navarre, and Armagnac were some of the names Jeanne had learned as she studied geography.

"It is all that used to be Gascony," Monsieur Bourbon said, "and a most delightful area."

Jeanne agreed with him. She enjoyed traveling in the big, brown coach to Navarre. She loved to bounce on the soft upholstered leather seats. And there was so much to see outside. Everywhere farmers, stripped to the waist, were working out of doors. Many were digging around the feet of orange and lemon trees, taking out the surface roots and the excess branches. From time to time cranes flew overhead. Birds sang in the trees, and Jeanne felt wonderful. She was going to see her papa and her maman, and surely it would be a glorious visit.

The castle-like château of Nérac, the capital of Albret, could be reached only by the wooden bridge over the Baise River. Surrounded by columns and sculptures, the château was impressive any day. But now, in the springtime with the sun glinting on its windows and turrets, it was especially so. As the horses' hooves rataplanned hollowly over the wood, Jeanne looked out at the great river below her. Upstream, over the water spuming across rocks, she could see a curiously shaped stone bridge. Beyond that lay the roofs of Nérac. After passing across the Baise River, a well-kept royal park spread out to her left. Jeanne recalled all these things from her last visit. The closer she came to the château the more excited she became, and she clapped her hands in delight at the huge fountain in the stone courtyard spraying crystal-clear water high into the air. The horses stopped, and the coachman opened the door for the little princess. Then she saw her mother, arms outstretched, and with a glad cry Jeanne ran headlong into her embrace.

There were a number of visitors at the château. They were older men, these visitors, and very clever. Jeanne had met Gérard Roussel before. He was Maman's almoner, and she had heard him preach. A kind man, he gravely bowed to her as, with a twinkle in his eye, he solemnly asked how Madame the Princess was doing. Then, to her great delight, he pulled a sweetmeat out of his pocket, which he presented as a treat. There was also Monsieur Jean Cauvin. He was a tall, very thin man who did not smile overly much. But she liked him anyway because he seemed awkward, ill at ease, and rather in need of a friend. She often tried to catch his eye and smile at him. When he noted this, he instantly smiled back, and then his whole long, severe face was transformed with gentleness. Then there was Monsieur Farel, a red-haired fireball of a man, who never sat still in Maman's salon but constantly fidgeted, ever walking about, gesturing as he talked and talking as he gestured. But Jeanne's favorite guest was a very old man, Monsieur Jacques Lefèvre d'Étaples. She loved Monsieur d'Étaples. Like a grandfather he would often take her on his lap and speak to her of Jesus and His very great love for those who were His children.

Early one morning as Jeanne ran into her mother's room, there were two visitors present, Monsieur Roussel and Monsieur Farel. Jeanne was eager to have Maman come and walk about the gardens with her. She had lately discovered that she liked birds very much and was anxious to show off her ability to imitate some of the calls they made. Monsieur Roussel and Monsieur Farel did not seem of a mind to leave quickly.

"Maman," Jeanne began several times, but each time her mother hushed her. So she sat down in a corner, sulking and comforting herself with the thought that Maman had, after all, promised to walk with her and that she would, at some point, have to keep her promise.

"How very sad these times are, Madame Marguerite!"

Monsieur Roussel's voice broke as he spoke. Jeanne watched her mother stride across the room and put her hand on Monsieur Roussel's shoulder.

"You are safe here, Monsieur! You need not fear or—"

"I know. I know. But the others!" Monsieur Roussel interrupted, continuing in a soft voice. "There has been so much bloodshed! And I have not been a good pastor. Often I held back!"

Monsieur Farel stood up. In spite of her impatience to be out of doors, the man fascinated Jeanne. He pounded on Maman's heavy oak table, making a fearful racket. His eyes glittered and, after pounding the table again with his fist, he too strode over to Monsieur Roussel.

"Well, Gérard! Go back then! Go back to Paris and join the martyrs, if you must speak in such a manner—as if there is no hope!"

He walked back to the table and pounded again. Jeanne wondered that his hand was not shattered.

"But there is hope!"

Monsieur Farel punctuated these last words by clapping his right hand into his left. Monsieur Roussel did not answer. Maman smiled faintly. A sad smile, but it was a smile indeed. Jeanne was somewhat relieved to see it.

"Gentlemen, I think it is time for prayer. Monsieur Farel, will you lead us, if you please?"

She motioned for Jeanne to come closer. Jeanne stood up, shaking the wrinkles out of her green gown. Her body stitchet felt tight and she breathed uneasily. Monsieur Farel knelt down in the middle of the room, and Monsieur Roussel knelt down next to him. Maman knelt down with them, motioning again for Jeanne to approach as well. Cautiously she knelt next to her mother, hindered somewhat by Marguerite's full skirt. It was strangely quiet now. A sparrow sang somewhere outside, and Jeanne thought that this was perhaps a prayer as well, only the bird did not need to kneel.

"Our Father Who art in heaven . . ." Monsieur Farel's voice began slowly but gathered quickly in volume and speed.

"We bring before Your Almighty throne the problems we have. It was but yesterday that we walked the streets in Paris where many of our brothers and sisters were killed. We know many who have died. We know scores who have endured cruel deaths. We lived among them, sat at their tables, and had converse with them. And now they have been slaughtered!"

Monsieur Farel's voice rose. It was quite loud now and terrible to hear. It reminded Jeanne of thunder and lightning. She edged as close to her mother as the skirt would permit.

"Our comfort, O Lord, is knowing that our brothers and sisters now wear white robes. Their martyrdom is a blazing torch which shall set all Europe afire with the knowledge of Your cause."

Monsieur Farel paused, and Monsieur Roussel coughed. In the corridor outside her mother's apartments, Jeanne thought she heard noise.

Monsieur Farel continued. "Your name, O Lord, will shine from the east to the west of all Christendom. It will—"

In the midst of his prayer the door was almost flung off its hinges. Jeanne's eyes, like the door, opened wide. She saw her father standing in the entrance, scowling.

Henri of Navarre was a dashing and handsome fellow even in anger. Tall and muscular, a black moustache curled disdainfully over red lips. His full, dark beard, just a little unkempt, covered a square, resolute chin. A fine-chained medallion hung over his broad shoulders. Jeanne could see the dark hairs just below the knuckles on her father's hand tremble. She shivered and awaited his displeasure. And that he was very displeased was evident by the redness of his cheeks and neck.

"What mean you, sirs," he bellowed at Messieurs Farel and Roussel, "to conduct Reformers' prayers here in my house?"

Monsieur Farel stood up, and Monsieur Roussel scrambled to his feet as well. Only Marguerite, the queen of Navarre, stayed down, seemingly calm and unruffled.

"They pray, sir, at my request," she said, her voice not shaking a bit.

Jeanne, filled with admiration for such a brave answer, turned to look at her. Her movement caused another outburst.

"And the child—she is here too? How you misform her, Madame. How you misshape her, to let her be present. Have you no thought of the future, woman?"

He strode over, breathing heavily as he strode, and his slashed sleeves flew about as he walked and gestured.

"And you sirs," he again roared at Messieurs Farel and Roussel, "out! Out! Out, I say!"

They left, nodding slightly to Marguerite as they went.

"Jeanne, come here!"

Jeanne stood up and faced her father. The veins in his square neck stood out, and she could see the heartbeat in them.

"Go and stand by the table."

She obeyed promptly. Her father's voice was not to be trifled with. As she walked over, she heard rather than saw the slap. Her father had hit her mother. She knew it to be a fact for when she turned, her mother's right cheek was turning a vivid red and her mother's face had an astonished and defensive look. In an instant she was back at her mother's side.

"Do not hit, Maman!"

"What! You would double your sin of misconduct by speaking out against me, your father?"

She could feel his hot breath as he bent over to speak to her. His hands reached out and closed tightly around her middle. Then he picked her up by the waist and carried her back to the table. There, putting his foot on a chair, he draped her like a cloth over his knee and took out a cane. Pulling away her skirt, he thoroughly beat the child who clenched her fists and cried. But no one came to help. When he was done, he put her down on the floor in front of him.

"Never, Jeanne, let me catch you praying with that lot again. Never, you understand?"

She looked at him, her face streaked with tears, her hair in tangles, and could not speak for the sobs that shook her. And all the while Marguerite said nothing but just stood holding her cheek. It suddenly struck Jeanne in all this that her father's velvet Basque cap was still perched jauntily on his head, and she thought that no matter how nice one might look, it was not one's outward appearance that told the story. No, one's outward appearance told you nothing at all.

5

WEDDING RUMORS

It was at Lonray, away from the pleasure-seeking court life and the decadent fashions paraded by many of the ladies there, that the child Jeanne grew. In her world of lesson plans with Aymée, there was order and decorum. She learned to ride a longhaired pony and studied history; she became more fluent in Latin and read French literature; and she played both backgammon and the lute. She also accompanied Aymée when she visited sick people in and around Lonray. It was one of Aymée's duties as a noblewoman, and it taught the princess that not all people wore lace ribbons or ate sweetmeats as a treat.

Every now and then Jeanne was invited to Alençon, just northeast of Lonray. It belonged to her mother, and before each visit Aymée schooled her in manners.

"Make sure you eat slowly at the great table and do not talk while you are eating."

Jeanne would nod. She knew she would not be dismissed until Aymée was done.

"Do not slurp your soup and never leave the spoon in the dish."

Jeanne nodded again without hearing what Aymée had actually admonished.

"And," the governess added, warming to her subject, "do not belch or lean on the table or pick your nose, Jeanne."

Jeanne grinned.

"I won't, Aymée," she always promised dutifully.

There was, it seemed, so much to learn. Jeanne took in all the lessons. And by the age of nine she had grown as tall as Aymée's shoulder.

In the summer the Lonray household was usually astir before daybreak. Servants got up with the rooster's crowing. Rising from their pallets in both the attic and the kitchen, some left for the fields, singing at the top of their voices. Others lighted the fires and began the kitchen chores. In her bedroom Jeanne would lie awake and wait for Yvette to come and bring her clothes—clothes she would first warm on a clothing rack in front of the fire. After she helped Jeanne take off her long nightgown, Yvette would pull a long chemise over the girl's head. Then Jeanne would wash her hands and face in a basin of cold water before putting on her dress and stockings. In winter, her dress would be wool or camlet, a fabric woven from camel or goat's hair. In summer, her dress would be fine silk such as samite, serdal, or damask. Many of Jeanne's and Aymée's dresses were trimmed with squirrel, lambskin, rabbit, fox, or ermine.

There was talk, or, to be more accurate, there were whispers in both the great hall and the kitchen. They were about Jeanne, and she was painfully aware of them because Yvette never hesitated about passing on backstairs gossip.

"Charles V of Spain wants his son, Philip, to marry you," Yvette reported while she vigorously brushed Jeanne's long, brown hair one night. "He has asked your uncle, the king, if this is agreeable to him."

Jeanne shrugged her shoulders. She had studied Spain in her geography lessons, and she was also learning the Spanish language. But she did not know Philip and she did not like the sound of his name. The thought of leaving Lonray, where she knew all the nooks and crannies of the house, made her feel queasy. Everyone knew that Spain was hot and dusty and that the people there were not at all as nice as the French people. She shrugged her shoulders again.

"It is not true," she said quietly, but she was not at all sure and did not sleep well that night.

When she confronted Aymée with the rumor, the matter was verified. It was true. Her uncle, King François, was considering a Spanish alliance.

"But I am not yet ten years old!" Jeanne said, wishing for the first time that she were six again.

"The marriage," Aymée explained, "will ensure a lasting friendship between France and Spain. Together they will be able to stand against the world."

"What is the world?" Jeanne asked, pressing her small, straight nose against the window.

To her the garden, the birds, and the beauty of the Lonray sky were the hub of the universe. She had no desire to rule or be anywhere else.

"Think of the gowns, the kirtles, the petticoats, the linens, the fine kerchiefs, the rails, the sleeves, and the fine biggens you might choose if you became a princess of Spain!"

Aymée tempted her, almost out of breath with the long list. Jeanne's nose wrinkled in distaste at Aymée's words.

"I do not want those things," she said with certainty.

On Jeanne's visits to the royal court at Blois she had never been impressed with the ladies' fine clothing or their elaborate new hairstyles. She much preferred to walk quietly in the magnificent gardens around the palace and to study the immense variety of flowers in them. Above all, she loved to listen to the birds and to watch their flight in the skies, either singly or as they flocked to some drinking place.

"But you would be a great princess! Just think of what you might be able to do!"

Aymée's words ended with a sigh because she knew that nothing she said would entice Jeanne. The child had never shown any desire for pomp or glitter or show. Although she appreciated fine paintings and sculptures, she was much more likely to go into raptures over a long-tailed squirrel than a precious necklace.

"Their Majesties, your royal mother and father," Aymée went on, as she rose to stand next to Jeanne, "are very joyful about this proposed match. They know that Spain would probably cede Lower Navarre to them. Think of it, Jeanne! Lower Navarre has not been in the possession of the Albret family since 1512. Your father has prayed for such a moment as this his whole life."

"Yes," Jeanne's reply was not slow in coming. "I know my father would rather have Lower Navarre in his pocket again than anything else. He dreams of it constantly."

"It may not mean that much to you, Jeanne," Aymée went on, "but remember that your father became king of Navarre when he was only fourteen years old. He saw his parents grieve deeply because they had lost this property to Spain; and he also watched them die in their struggle to regain it."

Jeanne thoughtfully played with the tassel on her kirtle.

"Well," Aymée continued, happy that Jeanne was not arguing with her, "the Spanish Emperor only asks two million *livres* for the whole territory, *if* you marry Philip. Of course two million *livres* is a lot of money, but money is cheaper than lives. It could be done. Think of it, Jeanne, just think of it! Your father would get his territory back without war or bloodshed."

Jeanne nodded, and unconsciously her right hand crept to her back. Although several years had passed, she still distinctly remembered where the bruises had been when her father had thrashed her.

"The thing is not yet done," she answered Aymée quietly.

Jeanne was right. The thing was not yet done. Her uncle lost his interest in the Spanish marriage. He remembered that Charles V had imprisoned him after the Battle of Pavia. And he also considered the fact that if his brother-in-law Henri regained control of Lower Navarre, he would become more powerful. So he hemmed and hawed, saying neither yes nor no. Finally Jeanne's father decided to take matters into his own hands. He secretly wrote Charles V a letter saying how pleased he would be to have his small daughter Jeanne marry Philip. But the letter was intercepted by King François and interpreted as treason against France.

As a precaution against further intrigue with Spain, the king and queen of Navarre were deprived of the guardianship of their daughter. Jeanne was taken away from Lonray, the only home she had ever known, and settled at a château in Plessis-Les-Tours. From now on she would be under her uncle's supervision. Aymée and many of the staff were permitted to go to Plessis with Jeanne, but visits with the king and queen of Navarre were restricted. Her uncle was quite determined that they would no longer be able to use her as a pawn to bargain with Spain.

6

ILLNESS

Plessis-Les-Tours was a grim place. Seen from a distance it looked lonely and forbidding, not at all the kind of place in which a young girl should grow up. A freestone high wall, with many iron-pronged spits masoned into it, surrounded the château. And a deep moat, furnished with a portcullis and drawbridge, surrounded the wall. Even though there was a wide and open courtyard, Jeanne shuddered the first time she saw the château. She so loved birds, and immediately noted that there were very few windows at Plessis—and each window had an iron grille in front of it as a barrier.

From the beginning she did not feel at home. Picking at her food and disinterested in her lessons, she began to lose weight. She hated the arguments that usually accompanied the infrequent visits from her parents. Her father would go on and on about an alliance with Spain, and her mother would disagree and talk about loyalty to Uncle Francois. Neither of them ever asked what Jeanne would like. At night, even when she burrowed under the covers like a small rabbit, she could not sleep. Lonely thoughts tumbled about in her small mind and echoed with the sad refrain that nobody really wanted her for herself.

Jeanne was ten years old now and, although not tall for her age, had a royal appearance. Her light-brown hair pulled away from a high, smooth forehead and was usually hidden under a cap. Her eyebrows curved in a pleasant arch, almost as if someone had delicately penciled them in. Her gray eyes could sparkle with glee. Her nose was straight and finely shaped. And her red lips were still childishly round but sweetly determined.

As the weeks at Plessis turned into months, it became increasingly evident that Jeanne was very unhappy. She pined for the familiar Lonray surroundings, from the great rooms and the lively kitchen, to the bed she had slept in from babyhood. She yearned to hear the quaint creaking of the rafters overhead in her old bedroom ceiling, eventually coming down with a bad case of homesickness. Aymée did her best. She put a hold on lessons, allowed riding at all hours of the day, and told stories. But Jeanne only grew more and more unhappy. Looking at the pale child quietly staring off into the distance, Aymée thought a trip to Blois might help. Some sixty kilometers northeast of Plessis, Blois lay within the permitted boundaries of Jeanne's outings. She knew Marguerite was there and thought it quite probable that Jeanne would cheer up in her mother's presence.

Rooks noisily flying about the old castle tower of Blois greeted Jeanne and Aymée upon their arrival. Ivy clung to the ramparts. Jeanne, usually keen on any birds she noted, made no comment on the black birds cawing overhead. She had leaned heavily against her governess during the last hour of the boat trip up the Loire.

"My head aches. I am so tired, Aymée."

Servants scurried to find a litter and immediately carried the child to a large and well-furnished apartment. They tucked Jeanne away under heavy blankets, and Marguerite's doctor was called for. He prescribed total rest. Aymée faithfully sat by the little girl's bedside. Jeanne tossed and turned with a high fever. She did not know where she was and plaintively cried for her nurse, Toinette. In her delerium she also began to sing a long-ago lullaby from her baby days.

When Jeanne was born, her grandmother, Louise of Savoy, had written down her own motto for the child, and these words had been carved deeply into her wooden cradle: "God gave me wings! I shall fly and come to rest."

Before she was a year Jeanne had sung the words along with her wet-nurse, Toinette, as a lullaby. Her childish treble, milk dribbling down a chubby chin, loudly chirped alongside Toinette's more mature one.

"Dieu m'a donné des ailes! Dieu m'a donné des ailes! Je volerai—je volerai et me reposerai."

Toinette had laughed and clapped her hands, swaying back and forth with amazement at such a precocious child. Not walking yet, but singing, to be sure.

"Dieu m'a donné!"

Toinette usually began the song again, and Jeanne, copying her, laughed and clapped her hands. She had the exquisite delight a child has when she has the full attention of a mother, albeit a foster mother.

"Dieu m'a donné des ailes," her cracked and feverish voice began, *"Je volerai . . ."*

As the fever rose Jeanne's voice dissolved. Toinette disappeared. Now the windows of Tours haunted her dreams, and she frantically tried to grope past them as she plucked at the woolen blankets on her bed. But always, always the bars in front of them stopped her and held her back. "Prisoner," they mouthed at her. "You are a prisoner, Jeanne of Navarre, and you will never, ever leave here."

Marguerite, after the initial surprise of having her child come to Blois, became a constant visitor at the bedside. Taking turns with Aymée, she bathed her daughter, fed her, and spoke to her. Jeanne's small hunched form under the mounds of covers awoke a maternal love. A feeling of guilt overwhelmed her, but she told herself that she had been too busy to see much of her little daughter. Even now as she sat at Jeanne's bedside, a letter lay in her lap from François, summoning her to the court in Paris. But she could not, at this point, bring herself to leave Jeanne to the care of others. She called for a paper and ink and began a reply.

"Monseigneur," she penned to her brother as she simultaneously kept an eye on her daughter. "Not for so small a matter as the illness of my daughter would I give you the trouble of reading a letter . . ."

She stopped. François had angered her lately. After all, he had done nothing to help recover Lower Navarre. Yet, in spite of this, she could not stop loving him. She continued her letter:

At the beginning Jeanne's fever was so high and her looseness of bowels with blood was so fast and furious that we feared for her life. If God had not brought down her fever after twenty-four hours her little body would have had more than it could stand. Tomorrow will be the fifth day of her illness. This morning she took some rhubarb and I find that it has helped.

Jeanne moaned, and Yvette emerged from the shadows of the canopied bed to place a cool cloth on the little girl's forehead. Marguerite waved her away and stood up to wipe Jeanne's face herself. The child opened her eyes and, seeing her mother, smiled a tiny smile. It was more than enough for Marguerite. It was almost, she thought to herself, as if she were young again and nursing her brother François. He'd had bouts of fever as well, and he'd smiled at her too in the same artless way. Jeanne closed her eyes again. Marguerite sat down, picked up the unfinished letter and bit the end of her quill. She was filled with love, both for Jeanne and for her brother, but now more for her brother.

I hope that He who put Jeanne in this world to be of service to you will give her grace to fulfill the desire of mother, father and herself, which is rather to see her dead than commit any deed against your intention. On this I base my hope of her recovery, because I have a firm faith that those who love you cannot perish.

Marguerite nursed Jeanne for two weeks and slowly the child recovered. The best medicine was Marguerite's attention. She relished the bedside talks, the spoon-fed broth, and the cool, gentle kiss she received each time her mother came and left.

"I must return to Fontainebleau." Marguerite spoke hesitantly, hands folded sedately in her lap as she sat by Jeanne's side.

The ever-present tears, which the still weak girl could not control, rolled down thin cheeks.

"You must not cry, ma chérie. I cannot help it. Your Uncle François has already written twice and . . ."

She stopped to wipe Jeanne's cheeks.

"Come, don't cry. You are doing very well. And you will never guess what I have for you. It's a present! A wonderful present! Something you may take back with you to Tours."

At the mention of the château, Jeanne's face clouded even more.

"I don't want to go back there. It's a sad place. It is a prison, I—" She stopped and looked at her mother appealingly.

"Come, come. Remember what your fine teacher, Monsieur Bourbon always says: 'Any difficulty can be overcome by careful work.' "

Jeanne did not reply but lay her head back on the pillow.

"Well, do you not want to see what it is that I have gotten for you?"

"Yes."

Jeanne's voice was small and almost a breath. She eyed the ceiling with great concentration. Inside her there were sobs, sobs as large as the frescoes on the wall and as wet as the rain in the dark clouds she could see drifting by through the window. If she tried to talk, surely she would howl like Noir when her puppies had been taken away, and then Maman would be angry. The truth was that happiness never lasted, never. Another tear rolled down her cheek. Marguerite sighed, stood up, and wiped the little trickle with a cloth, speaking brightly as she did so.

"Well, then, I will get your present and you will see what it is."

She left the room and returned a little later. Jeanne could hear some bustling in the hall and in spite of herself was curious. Her mother smiled and reached out a hand toward her.

"Will you sit up in a chair for a while?"

Jeanne neither answered nor took her mother's hand, but watched the door. There was increasing noise beyond it.

"Well," her mother withdrew her hand and sat down again by the bed, "I suppose then that you can stay in bed."

She motioned to Yvette who went to open the door. A man entered. Jeanne knew him at once. It was Clément Marot, a poet, and her mother's secretary. He was a quiet man, but a very genial person, someone who sometimes wrote verses to cheer her. She smiled at him, and he bowed.

"Madame Jeanne."

Then he looked at her mother questioningly. Marguerite nodded, and Monsieur Marot returned to the door, extending his head into the corridor and calling out.

Then he stood aside, and another man entered. She did not know this man, but it was obvious from his appearance that he was a peasant. As he walked over to the bed, she saw that the peasant carried something on his shoulder, something that moved. Jeanne suddenly sat up, straining her eyes to see what it was. It was a small animal. A little brown and wizened face peered out at her from his spot next to the man's curly black hair. The man bowed exaggeratedly as the animal clung to his neck. In her excitement Jeanne forgot to greet him.

"What is it? What is that animal?"

Jeanne's cheeks grew red and her voice became animated. Her mother and Monsieur Marot laughed.

"It is a monkey," Marot answered, "a rhesus monkey, to be exact. And he has come to be your playmate."

"Mine. He is for me?"

Jeanne's voice squeaked. Her fingers crumpled the sheets on her bed in excitement. Upon a sign from Marguerite, the man stepped even closer to the bed. The monkey's arm companionably rubbed his head, knocking his cap askew.

"What is his name?"

Jeanne could hardly contain her excitement.

"Whatever name you choose to give him, Your Royal Princess," the man said, "that name is his. But I've always called him Henri."

"Henri! Why, that's the same name as Papa!"

Marguerite laughed out loud.

"But that will never do, Jeanne. You must name him again, I'm afraid."

Jeanne considered the monkey, who nonchalantly lounged on the man's shoulder, his slender body resting against his head. The animal's hair seemed to be standing straight up on its tiny brown-colored head.

"Can I see it closer?" she asked politely, and the man reached up and tossed the animal down, none too gently, on the bed.

Gray prickly chest and stomach hairs came jumping down on Jeanne. A small mouth chattered indignantly near her own. She shivered for a moment with the newness of this small creature, but then overcame her fear and stroked its back. It regarded her with its dark eyes, squinting a bit. Its long tail wrapped companionably around her hand. She felt the warm furriness on her skin. It was almost like the monkey was saying, "How do you do and do you like me?" She smiled.

Its little brown hand tentatively touched her hair, and she sat very quietly.

"Well, Jeanne, what shall you name it?" Her mother looked at her inquiringly.

She shrugged, and the monkey, suddenly fascinated by the curtained hangings around the bed, jumped from her side and clung to them, beginning a swinging climb upward. The man immediately grabbed it before it was able to clamber too high, and everyone laughed uproariously. The monkey clung to the man again, wrapping his arms around the square neck, kissing him on the cheek. The man affectionately returned the kiss while he rubbed the monkey's smooth back.

"What does it eat?" Jeanne asked, anxious that this time should last and that the monkey be well taken care of.

The man continued to caress the monkey, who now insolently took the man's cap off, placing it on his own head, grimacing and showing all his teeth as he did so. The man took the cap back, scolding him even as he cradled him tenderly. He loved the creature, that was plain. Then he answered Jeanne.

"Oh, mostly fruit and leaves."

"That shouldn't be too hard, should it, Maman? Can it stay in the room here with me now, please, Maman?"

"No, but tomorrow, when we travel back to Plessis, it will be on the boat and you can play with it then."

At the mention of Plessis, Jeanne's face fell. She had for a moment forgotten that she must return to what she referred to as her prison. She had forgotten for a moment that she was a princess, after all, and not a common peasant child who might come and go as she pleased in the village where she lived.

7
RETURN TO PLESSIS

"There are galleries at Tours, many more than there are here at Blois. Jeanne will be able to get the proper exercise. It is much better for her there."

Marguerite was arguing with Aymée as they were boarding the boat that was to take them down the Loire from Blois back to Plessis-Les-Tours. Clément Marot, who was to come along, walked about on the deck. Jeanne was already aboard, wrapped in soft blankets and settled on a long chair. But in spite of all the good care, she appeared miserable and downcast. Marot sat down next to her.

"Come, come, Madame la Princesse, you must smile a bit. A cheerful, smiling heart is like good medicine. Do you not know that a smile always makes the blood run warmer and that one's very bones salute when you smile?"

To illustrate his words, Marot gave Jeanne a huge grin and then stood up and saluted her. She managed to give him a thin smile but could not keep tears from forming in her eyes as he again took his place beside her.

"I do not want to go to Plessis, Monsieur Marot. I truly do not."

"Well, there are worse places to go to, you know. For example, what if you had to go to . . ."

He stopped for a moment and thought carefully.

"Well, what if you had to go to . . ."

He scratched his head in a somewhat perplexed manner, and Jeanne laughed in spite of herself.

"You see there are no worse places, Monsieur Marot."

"Yes," he countered, gladdened by her smiles, "I know there are worse places than Plessis. I just know it. Suppose, for example, you had to go to classes with Monsieur Bourbon right now and do mathematics all day long. Eh? How about that one?"

He looked at her triumphantly and continued. "Or what if you had to go to the jungle to live with the elephants. How about that?"

She almost giggled now. "Oh, Monsieur Marot. You are funny."

He grinned, satisfied that he had made her look somewhat happy again. "Or what if you had to go to a convent to live with the long-faced nuns?"

He put a hand over his face, and when he took it away, his face was very somber and most bleak. Jeanne now laughed out loud, and the oarsmen pushed off with the boat, setting course down river.

It was not until the afternoon that she remembered the monkey.

"Where is the little creature?" Marguerite asked Marot when Jeanne questioned her.

Marot looked down at the deck. He did not respond. Marguerite repeated the question, and he seemed embarrassed. Coughing into his hand, he began to speak softly.

"I can't hear you, Monsieur Marot," Jeanne called out. "Whatever happened to my monkey? I would like to play with him now, I think, and I have also decided on a name for him. Larat—I shall call him Larat. I thought last night that the fur on his back rather seemed like Father Larat's habit. What do you think, Mother?"

Marguerite smiled.

"I think it is a rather hopeful name for the creature, Jeanne. Do you think it will ever be as clever as Father Larat?"

Aymée clucked disapprovingly.

"You two mustn't make fun of Father Larat. No matter what you think of the man, he is still a priest and as such, a servant of God."

"Oh, Aymée! Father Larat is about as good an example of a cleric as Marot here is a good example of a soldier."

Jeanne laughed, remembering Marot's silly salute that morning. She looked up at him to see how he liked this joke but was startled to see that he appeared very uncomfortable.

"Maman did not mean," she began, but he waved his hand to stop her.

"No, ma petite Princesse, it is not what your Maman said. It is . . . It is . . ."

"The monkey," she filled in, "something happened to the monkey?"

He nodded.

"Alas, yes. The man who brought him up to your suite yesterday turned out to be less than honest. After he was paid for the little animal and, I might add, paid rather handsomely, he disappeared. The monkey was locked up in a cage, but the cage was open this morning and no trace of either monkey or owner could be found."

Jeanne was silent. She remembered how the curious little animal had thrown his arms around the man and kissed him. She knew the man loved the monkey. Strangely enough she bore him no malice for taking the animal back.

"It is no sin to love. I think," she said at length, "the man could not bear to be separated from his pet because he loved him so much."

She looked at her mother as she spoke. It seemed strange that the man probably loved that ugly little monkey more than her mother loved her. The menace of staying at Plessis loomed large again, and everything connected with it seemed to be designed for unhappiness. Marguerite made no comment but gazed out at the dark river for a long while before she spoke.

"I was going to surprise you when we landed, ma petite, but I will tell you now of another gift that I have for you."

"Another surprise?"

Jeanne's voice was low and without enthusiasm. She thought nothing would ever lift her spirits again.

"Yes, I have another surprise!"

Even Aymée's attention was caught by the sudden, playful lilt in Marguerite's voice.

Marguerite continued, "I have bought a parrot, and he will be waiting for you at Plessis-Les-Tours."

"A parrot?"

"Yes, and I know that this parrot will be in a cage when you arrive and that no one will be able to steal him away. Only yesterday I spoke to the fellow who delivered him, and he assured me the bird had arrived safely."

"What color is he?"

"Green."

"What happened to my birds at Alençon? The ones you gave me there, Maman?"

Jeanne owned six turkey cocks and six hens at her mother's château at Alençon, birds to which she was very much attached. She had often fed them in the park when she visited there. They were her special pets.

"Pierre Beauschune, the caretaker, he will mind them, Jeanne, and he will bring some of their eggs to the Ave Maria convent at Alençon—"

She did not get any farther.

"But I asked for them to be brought to Plessis. Why can't . . ." Jeanne's words dissolved into sobs.

"Oh, ma petite, King François forbade the taking of the birds to Plessis. He did not allow me to . . ."

"I hate Uncle François! He is not kind."

The oarsmen stopped rowing. Jeanne had arrived back at Plessis-Les-Tours.

8

A History Lesson

Plessis-Les-Tours was built of brick and rose two stories high. Constructed around three sides of a court, its corners had forbidding iron watchtowers. Although Plessis looked grim on the outside, the inside was surprisingly comfortable. Spacious and simple, the rooms held many beautiful paintings, something Jeanne truly appreciated. Most of the rooms also contained stone angels—angels about three feet tall and holding scrolls. Jeanne would stand in front of them and speak to them when she was bored.

"So, how long have you been here?"

Then she would grimace and answer herself.

"Yes, much longer than I have, I know. So long you've actually turned to stone."

Then, pirouetting about, just to prove to them that she was not made of stone, she would dance around their still forms. The angels always gazed at her without any expression and just stood in their splendid painted costumes of gold and azure. The inscription on every single scroll they held was the same:

Misericordias Domini in Eternum Cantabo, I will forever sing the mercy of God.

Through the grille on a second-story window Jeanne gazed at the forest beyond Plessis.

"If I ever marry and have children," she said to Aymée, "I shall love them very much."

On her knees in a window seat, she looked out at the surrounding countryside.

As an afterthought, she added, "And if I had a brother, I would not love him better than I loved my children."

It remained quiet in the room. Glancing at Aymée who was not responding but concentrating on her needlework, Jeanne said, "And I do believe I hate Uncle François."

"It is wrong to hate," Aymée answered automatically as she threaded silk gold thread on her needle for the embroidery work in front of her.

Satisfied to have her governess finally acknowledge that she was speaking, Jeanne slid off the window seat and sat down by Aymée's feet.

"Tell me again, Aymée. About Pavia, I mean. Because it was after this battle that Maman married Papa."

She stopped, unsure of what it actually was that she wanted to know. She had heard the story of the battle many times before, not only from Aymée, but also from her tutor, from Monsieur Jouanne, and from the servants.

Aymée sighed and stroked Jeanne's hair.

"Many people died at Pavia. You know the story, child." The governess spoke softly, recalling her chivalrous husband as she always did when she spoke of Pavia. If he had lived . . . If only he had lived . . . Well then she would probably not be sitting here now with the eleven-year-old princess of Navarre.

"Well?"

Jeanne's voice cut into Aymée's reflections and Aymée shook her head to clear her thoughts. She began matter-of-factly.

"The Battle of Pavia, as you well know, was fought in Italy. It was only one battle in the ongoing war between the ruling houses of France and Austria. Your uncle wanted, and rightly so, a balance of power in Europe, and Charles V wanted to rule the world. Well, in any case," Aymée sighed, "your uncle, King François, was captured by the Emperor Charles and imprisoned."

Jeanne snickered at this and wiggled her toes.

"I'll wager he did not like it, being a prisoner. And that is one thing my father, Henri of Navarre, bested him in, isn't it? For my father was in the battle too, but he escaped from prison."

"Do you wish me to tell the story or not?"

Jeanne was silent and looked up half-remorsefully and half-mischievously at her governess.

"Please go on, Aymée," she said.

"Your maman and grandmaman were distraught. The noblest army France had ever sent forth had been annihilated in Italy. Many nobles had been killed. My husband, God rest his soul, and Monsieur d'Alençon, to whom your mother was married at that time, both died."

"Monsieur d'Alençon, he was a coward, n'est-ce-pas?"

"Yes, indeed, so it was said but not—"

"I know. I know," Jeanne interrupted, "not your husband. He was brave and fine and good."

Aymée remained silent until Jeanne apologized.

"I am sorry, my Aymée. Indeed, you must miss him."

Aymée swallowed and continued.

"The excitement in Paris over the king's capture was fearful. There was panic everywhere. People worried the city would not be safe. But your grandmaman, Louise of Savoy, kept her head and devised measures for the safety of Paris. Only five gates were kept open, a constant guard was maintained, troops were recalled from where they had scattered and prayers were offered up in the churches."

"Which helped the most, do you suppose, Aymée?" Jeanne asked. "The prayers or the safety measures Grandmaman devised?"

Aymée paid her no heed and made as if to continue. But Jeanne interrupted.

"I do not mean to make fun of the church, Aymée. But I know, for you have told me, of the procession my uncle walked in by the Abbey of Saint-Denis."

To illustrate her words, Jeanne got up and marched around the table.

"So my uncle marched before the battle in his royal robes. His sword was carried, unsheathed, by the Constable. The scepter was carried by . . ."

She paused and then went on.

"I've forgotten who carried the scepter. And someone else carried his crown."

Aymée nodded and Jeanne continued.

"And then they prayed devoutly in the Abbey for victory. So why," she ended rather fiercely as she stood by the table, "why did they lose, Aymée? Was God not with my uncle? Or was it not proper for him to go to war?"

Aymée cleared her throat.

"The king's will was God's will. The king's cause was God's cause."

Jeanne shook her head. Aymée had not answered her questions.

"Yvette told me that Grandmaman said that the misfortune of Pavia was the fault of the Lutherans, those of the new religion, and that she then made a vow to kill them. But I cannot understand why Uncle François's losing a battle in Italy was the fault of the Lutherans. What do you think, Aymée?"

"You must ask your father the next time he visits."

Aymée now, as always, refused to be goaded into an argument. Jeanne made a face. As if she would ask her father about Lutherans or any Reformers after the thrashing he had given her at Nérac.

"I might ask my mother," she said, "for I know that she protects and often meets with those of the new religion. She does well in this, my mother, but why does she not also meet with me more often? I know Uncle François would give her permission if she asked."

It bothered Jeanne immensely that she saw so little of her parents. Every now and then, if she was ill, Marguerite might hasten down for a spell of nursing or, if she had a bit of time on her hands, would take Jeanne for a small holiday to some hot water spring known to be good for one's health.

"Your mother does what seems best to her."

Jeanne sighed, sat down at Aymée's feet again and relaxed. "Go on, tell me more."

Aymée continued her narrative.

"While negotiations were going on for the release of your Uncle François, he became ill. Your mother traveled to Spain to see him. It was a dangerous journey. She arrived in Barcelona and proceeded to Madrid. There the Emperor Charles V himself met her at the gates to escort her to her brother. Not waiting to change her clothes, even though she was dusty and tired, your mother mounted a palfrey and rode through the streets of Madrid at the right hand of the Emperor Charles V and his men. She showed no fear. The Emperor was overcome with respect for such devotion to a brother. When your mother was finally taken in to see your uncle, she found him at death's door. He wept when he saw her, but her presence so cheered him that he began to get better."

"I cannot imagine my uncle, the king of France, weeping."

Aymée paid no heed to the interruption and continued. "Your mother tried to manage an escape, but it failed."

"What happened?"

"Someone betrayed her plan, and your uncle was more closely guarded. Your mother was now in danger herself and began her journey back home to France, despite the fact that it was winter and the weather was very severe. In eight days she traveled a distance usually performed in twice the time, and at nightfall of the very day on which her safe conduct expired she reached Roussillon. Charles V's Spanish troops, who had been following her closely, saw her surrounded by a French force."

"You love my mother, don't you, Aymée?"

"She is brave and good."

"But she does not travel much to see me, or brave bad weather to spend time at Plessis with me, does she?"

Aymée didn't respond, and this angered Jeanne.

"Perhaps," she threw out, "my mother loves Reformers more than me, even as she loves her brother more than me. For she risks her life, doesn't she, to help them?"

There was only the noise of Aymée's somewhat labored breathing. Jeanne continued without waiting for a response.

"And why, I wonder, does my mother risk her life for the Reformers, for she herself is not of the new faith? Why does she do it, Aymée?

Aymée stopped sewing.

"It is difficult to explain," she said.

"Yes," answered Jeanne, "it must be. For you are not doing a very good job of it. Why does she not risk something for me? She could say to my uncle, 'Let Jeanne come home to Navarre. She is my daughter. She belongs with me and with her father.' "

Aymée bit her lower lip.

"You are being silly, Jeanne."

"And what about you, Aymée? You used to be at court all the time. And then you were demoted from lady-in-waiting to governess. I think you are not always pleased that my mother picked you for the job of minding me."

"Yes, I am."

Aymée's voice was low.

"But you don't really want to be here with me, do you?"

Instead of answering, Aymée bent back down over her sewing.

"I am a thing," Jeanne continued, "a thing my father wants to trade to the Emperor Charles so he can have Lower Navarre back and a thing my mother wants to trade to Uncle François so she can keep his favor." Her voice shook as she added, "I wonder if they really love me."

Aymée began to speak and then fell silent. Outside a horn sounded in the distance. Both Aymée and Jeanne got up and walked over to the window. Through its metal grating they could see a royal party approaching Plessis.

"It is probably Uncle François. It is a good thing he travels straight and not by any of the side lanes or his horses might step on some forgotten caltrop."

Jeanne, who had regained her composure somewhat, spoke flippantly, laughing up at Aymée. But she was trembling inside. What did her royal uncle want of her now? For it was a fact that when he came he usually had something up his royal sleeve.

9

BETROTHAL

It was not King François himself who arrived at Plessis but an armed escort with an order to take Jeanne to Fontainebleau immediately. Servants scurried, clothes were packed, and Aymée was flustered. But both Jeanne and her governess were ready and off the next morning, Jeanne waving an exaggerated goodbye to Yvette who was being left behind. Two days later, after an overnight stay at a hostelry, their carriage drove up Porte Dorée, the main entrance to Fontainebleau—the palace described by many people as "a new Rome."

Straightening up in her seat and steeling herself to meet Uncle François, Jeanne glanced out of the carriage window. A secluded path, still and inviting, led off Porte Dorée into a forest at her right hand.

"Look, Aymée," she pointed excitedly, "woods! Do you suppose there are a lot of birds here and that I might be able to walk there?"

Aymée smiled. She had her own thoughts as to this urgent visit but had not spoken to Jeanne about them. There had been talk about marriage again. This time the proposed suitor was a young duke from Clèves.

"Well?" Jeanne impatiently tugged at Aymée's sleeve. "What do you think? Might Uncle François, if I am very polite, let me walk about his forest?"

"Perhaps," Aymée answered softly, "perhaps if you are obedient to his wishes, His Majesty will consider letting you walk in the forest of Bière. He is fond of the hunt so maybe . . ."

"Oh, Aymée," Jeanne called out in a distressed voice, "you know that I care nothing for the hunt. I would like to walk about, that is all."

She ended abruptly. The horses had come to a halt. Aymée shook the crumples out of Jeanne's russet gown and bade her to smile.

Fontainebleau was the palace where François I felt most at home. Before he remodeled it, it had been an ancient hunting lodge. He preserved the solid foundations of the lodge and built the palace on top of them. Italian architects constructed elaborate apartments for François, his wife, and children. Galleries, a ballroom, chapels, a great staircase, and porticos— all pleased the eye and made the beholder gasp in wonder.

Jeanne looked about with amazement when she descended from the carriage. The sun had just set, and the reddish-purple streaks left behind in the sky cast a deceptive aura of peace on a magnificent courtyard filled with trees and fountains. Imposing buildings surrounded the courtyard. Many servants were lined up in front of them, wigged and ornately dressed. They all bowed low to the ground. Jeanne smiled at them cautiously. She was not accustomed to so many eyes on her at the same time and didn't like it one bit.

A steward led her up a marble staircase, Aymée following close behind. When they were almost at the top, Uncle François suddenly appeared out of nowhere. He was fashionably clad in puffed scarlet breeches, and his matching long-sleeved scarlet doublet was slashed to show slivers of gold lining. Smiling pleasantly, he held out his hand. Jeanne, well trained in the ways of etiquette, took it, bowing deeply before she kissed his fingers. Aymée attended the king in a similar manner.

"Well, Niece," the king's voice was jovial as he escorted them inside, "and how was your journey?"

"Long, Sire, and exceedingly dusty and tiresome."

Jeanne's voice was exasperated and worn. She had never been shy about expressing her feelings. François laughed heartily. It was a loud, infectious laugh, and several close attendants laughed with him.

"We must see to it then that you can bathe, change your clothes, and rest," he said.

He clapped his hand and a number of ladies stepped forward.

"I will see you, Jeanne, in some hours. Indeed, we will sup together, you and I."

Jeanne smiled politely. Whatever it was her uncle wanted of her would be broached at dinner.

She withdrew with the ladies to an apartment that had been made ready for her. After a hot bath she was dressed in a satin purple gown. Aymée said it would please her uncle. The gown trained upon the ground, its long lace sleeves trimmed with jet and pearl buttons cut back to show the purple velvet under-sleeves around her arms. Her shoes were made of Spanish leather. A velvet cap of the same color and material as her dress was carefully placed on her hair, and about her neck she wore a pomander chain. Aymée surveyed the end result with satisfaction.

"You look lovely, ma chérie."

There were three for dinner. Jeanne was surprised to find that her mother was also at Fontainebleau. They embraced formally. A number of paintings hung on the wall, and, ever interested in art, Jeanne wandered over to look at one whose beauty particularly struck her. Uncle François came to stand behind her.

"You like that one, ma petite?" he questioned lightly.

She nodded. The woman looking out at her from the frame wore an enigmatic smile. She was pale and seemed to be thinking deeply.

"It is the portrait of La Gioconda, the wife of a gentleman in Italy named Giocondo. Some people call this painting *Mona Lisa*. I was fortunate enough to buy it for only twelve thousand francs."

Jeanne stared at the painting a few moments longer.

"Who was the artist?" she asked at length.

"Leonardo da Vinci. I have five more of his works. Come, I will show you the others."

François walked Jeanne about the room, pointing out his da Vincis as well as his other paintings. In spite of herself, Jeanne was entranced. She loved art and could hardly be persuaded to sit down.

There were chickens, capons, partridges, and hare; there were venison pasties, veal pasties, and saltcellars made of gold; and there was sparkling, red wine poured into boat-shaped crystal cups. Jeanne drank slowly, clasping her small hands over her cup's crystal handles. She was not very hungry and fear gnawed at her insides. Maman was here, but Papa was not. It was likely that Uncle François wanted her to do something of which Papa would not approve. Uncle François pushed a basket brimming over with nuts toward her.

"Taste some of these, ma petite. You will like them."

She shook her head. "I have had enough. I thank you, Uncle François."

Uncle François pushed back his chair. Reaching over, he picked up a linen napkin, wiping his hands carefully. All the while from under drooping eyelids, he regarded Jeanne with a measured stare. She returned his gaze at first but then looked down with a tiny smile, amused by the thought that when people called Uncle François *le roi au long nez*, the king with the long nose, they were right.

"Ma petite," he began, and she thought, "Here it comes. This is why I was summoned."

"Ma petite," he repeated, and she stared, not at his face but at his elegant clothes. He had changed his scarlet doublet for another. This one was laced and braided, rich in gems and precious ornaments. His shirt was very white and peeked through the opening.

"You are getting older, and, as such, the matter of your marriage . . ."

She suddenly sat up very straight and tried to catch her mother's eye. But Marguerite was intent on her plate, toying with uneaten food.

". . . the matter of your marriage," Uncle François repeated, "is very dear to our hearts."

"I have no wish," she began, but Uncle François interrupted smoothly.

"No wish to do anything, no doubt, but that which pleases us."

He smiled at her, but her face remained rigid. He continued.

"The Duke of Clèves has asked for your hand in marriage."

He stopped and considered his nails, blunt and clean, and then began tapping his right hand repeatedly on the tablecloth. Jeanne was silent and again looked imploringly at her mother, but Marguerite would not catch her gaze.

"The Duke of Clèves, as you must know from your lessons with Monsieur Bourbon, is ruler of a significant duchy in the Rhine Valley. It pleases the Valois house," he paused, including his sister in the conversation, "our house of Valois, to strengthen the ties we have in the Germanies. Is that not so, Marguerite?"

At last Marguerite spoke, still avoiding Jeanne's eye.

"William de la Marck, the Duke of Clèves, is an admirable young man. He is twenty-four years old, and quite handsome, already proving himself an admirable ally of France."

"He is older than I am," said Jeanne slowly, her mind working hard at trying to figure out a way to make marriage seem unlikely, silly, and unreasonable.

"Tut, tut, child," her uncle answered, " that has nothing to do with it. And many girls as old as you are already betrothed or wed. Besides, the marriage contract has already been drawn up."

Marguerite unexpectedly smiled at her. It was such a warm smile that Jeanne's hopes soared. Was Maman going to help her after all? But the words that followed the smile were disappointing.

"You will get a new wardrobe, Jeanne. And, just think of it, you will be the Duchess of Clèves."

"I do not want . . ." Jeanne began.

But Uncle François interrupted her again. He spoke imperiously with a voice that brooked no defiance.

"You do not want to do anything but that which pleases us. That is what you wish to say, is it not so?"

His eyes were cold, and they narrowed as he spoke. It reminded her of the time when her father had beaten her in her mother's chambers for praying with the Reformers. Shivering as she recollected the scene, she yielded to the inevitable.

"I am content," she whispered at her plate.

"Content to do what?" Uncle François asked sharply.

"Content to do what you ask," she said.

He smiled and lifted his wineglass off the table. "I will drink to that, what do you say, ma soeur?"

But Marguerite, although she lifted up her glass to the toast, was quiet.

That night Jeanne cried herself to sleep.

10

PROTEST

Jeanne's father was furious when he heard what had happened—furious with Marguerite, François, and anyone who happened to be in his neighborhood. He had still hoped for a marriage between Jeanne and the Spanish Prince Philip; had still hoped for the recovery of Lower Navarre. Marguerite, who bore the brunt of her husband's anger, grew so distraught at his ill humor that she almost became ill.

"You have brought misfortune on the house of Albret, Madame," Henri bellowed at her in rage, "and you have conspired against me with your brother."

Jeanne had been sent back to Plessis. She was now betrothed to a duke, a man twice her age, who lived in the Germanies, in the far-away Duchy of Clèves. Through her curtained bedroom window, past the grille, the forlorn girl watched birds spread their wings and soar upward. In her heart she wished she could fly away as they did.

And so almost a year passed. Lessons went on with Monsieur Bourbon who continued to feed Jeanne Latin authors and French literature. But what she loved best of all were the times when she rode with Monsieur Perault, the stable master. He was a gentle, dependable man who knew much about animals. He often spoke to her as they rode, three grooms-men not far behind.

"Listen, Princess Jeanne," he would say as they passed fields in the early morning, "listen carefully and you will hear a thousand birds in chorus. Some," and he would point, "perch on the hedge over there, and others hide, waiting for the plow-man to plow so they can feed on the worms which come out of the freshly turned earth."

She would rein her horse in to a standstill and nod as she heard the birds twittering. Then they would smile at one another in perfect understanding.

"Do you know," he said one day, "that some birds flit here and there to show where there is a fox? Or to tell you what weather is approaching?"

Fleetingly she thought of Father Larat. Would birds flit here and there to tell people that he was hiding somewhere? She bit her lip to keep from grinning, lest Monsieur Perault might think she was laughing at him.

"How do they know, Master Perault?" she asked, and he, much pleased to be asked, answered readily.

"Why, I warrant God has told them, for they do know. For example, if you see a heron, motionless at the water's edge, that means winter is near. Other signs of winter are sheep running about hither and thither, or a jay going to roost earlier than usual."

"I don't like winter very much," said Jeanne. "Are there other signs also, Monsieur Perault? Maybe signs for . . . well, for rain?"

"Yes, truly, there are. A swallow skimming over water predicts rain, or, if he flies high, that means fine weather. And a green woodpecker never fails to sing before it rains."

"I never like to sing before it rains!"

Jeanne laughed merrily now as she stroked her horse's neck. Monsieur Perault laughed too.

"Neither do I," he confided, "but is it not a marvel how our good God has given all these little creatures such a sense of knowing. Listen the next time it rains, Princess, and if you happen to hear a hoot owl calling through the patter of the raindrops, it means clear weather is in the offing."

"You know so much," said Jeanne. "I wish that you could be with me during my lessons instead of Monsieur Bourbon. Though indeed," she hurried to add, not wishing to be unfair, "he is also full of knowledge and quite kind."

Jeanne also loved flowers. She had her own flowerbeds, which Aymée permitted her to work with the help of a gardener. Jeanne tended them with love, carefully staking plants top-heavy with blooms and faithfully raking the gravel paths between the beds. A small pond had also been dug for her pleasure and water lilies as well as goldfish gave her a great deal of joy.

"Look how the lilies open their mouths," she said to Aymée. "They sing to God for the very pleasure of being in the pond."

"Flowers do not sing," said Aymée, whose imagination never ran away with her.

They sat on a bench by a yew hedge, relaxing in the balm of a late spring afternoon. Jeanne had been coughing and Aymée wisely realized fresh air would be beneficial.

"Oh, but they do, Aymée," Jeanne replied, looking sideways at her governess and shielding her eyes from the glint of the west sun. "They have voices even as the pigeons coo and the blackbirds caw. It's just that you hear flowers' voices on your inside or sometimes you see their voices with your eyes. I am sorry if you have never heard or seen them. The indigo voice of the iris is sort of low, like Monsieur Jouanne's voice. The alyssum has a very pure sound, and the yellow marigold has a buttery, soft sound."

Aymée smiled tolerantly. Jeanne picked a daisy from the grass and twirled it about in her hand.

"Even this small flower has a voice. It says 'Alleluia! Alleluia!' "

Now Aymée shook her head. The child was too isolated. There was nothing lacking in her intelligence, but she was oversensitive.

"Yvette says," Jeanne went on, still twirling the little daisy, "that there is a priest in Beaumont somewhere who has his coffin set out in the vestry. He is not ill but every morning on his way to prayer, he makes a show of looking at it. It is to remind him, he says, of his coming death."

A frog croaked. Jeanne coughed and laughed all in one breath before she continued.

"Now there is a sound of life. I'll wager the frog does not think of death but rejoices in all the lily pads God has given him. That priest would do better to share his food and his drink and the love of God rather than pretend to be . . ."

"Pretend to be what?" Aymée asked.

"Well," Jeanne reflected, "it is easy to show off piety in words and by kneeling down in front of other people. But it seems to me that the heart of the matter is what one does afterward. Don't you think, Aymée?"

Aymée's answer was typical.

"God rewards good deeds, Jeanne. That is true."

A stable boy ran up the path. Bowing, he informed Madame de Lafayette that a messenger had arrived and was awaiting their pleasure in the *grande salle*.

The messenger came from Navarre. When he requested a private audience, Jeanne permitted him to retire with her and Aymée into a small anteroom. Here he whispered that he had a document, which her father wished her to sign. Aymée read the document over Jeanne's shoulder.

I here protest before you that I have no desire to marry the Duke of Clèves, and, as of now, I swear that I will never be his wife. If by chance I should promise to be his wife, it would be because I fear that King François will otherwise do harm to my father the king of Navarre. I make this protest in your presence so that you will be my witnesses. I sign this written protest and I beg you to sign it as witnesses.

"You would do well to obey," Aymée said.

Jeanne thought of the birds flying free up in the sky and immediately agreed. Without further ado, Aymée called her son-in-law and daughter, who were visiting Plessis, to be present as witnesses to Jeanne's signature —a childish script written in hope.

II

Threats

The truth is that documents signed by girls who are only just twelve years old, even when observed by witnesses, do not keep away kings and dukes. And so, not too much later in that early summer of 1541, King François paid a visit to his niece, taking the Duke of Clèves with him. He thought it high time Jeanne met her fiancé. Jeanne, who had a fever and was in bed at the time of the visit, received her uncle in her bedchamber. Kissing his hands, which he reached out to her, she thanked him for coming. He responded graciously.

"You look tired, ma petite. And no wonder. It has been raining for days. But soon, in full summer, you will be yourself again. And now, perhaps this evening, you can bestir yourself enough to rise from your bed to welcome the duke. Indeed, he is most anxious to meet you since the date for the marriage has been set for next month."

Jeanne felt herself grow cold in spite of the many blankets, which covered her.

"The duke is here? He is here today? But I cannot marry him, Uncle François."

Swallowing hard and pressing her head back on her pillow, she spoke bravely, firmly counting on the fact that even her uncle would not strike someone who was ill and in bed.

"You told me at Fontainebleau, while your mother was with us, that you were content to marry the duke. Why do you say no now? Who has told you to refuse?"

"When I replied to Your Majesty at Fontainebleau that I would marry the duke, I did not know it would displease my father. If Your Majesty wants me to marry, let me marry someone in France. I would rather enter a convent than marry the Duke of Clèves."

Jeanne's voice rose in courage and vehemence as she spoke. Her uncle's voice rose as well.

"I see you've been coached in what to say. Who told you it would not please your father?"

"A gentleman sent by some of my father's subjects."

François arose from his chair by the bed and began pacing the floor.

"Jeanne, you will do what you have promised to do."

"But, Sire, my father, the king of Navarre, does not want me to marry the duke."

"The marriage will take place, and if you will not marry the duke, you will be punished severely."

Aymée who had been standing on the other side of the bed, looked alarmed. Apprehensively she took a step backward. Suddenly noting the governess, the king now included her in his circle of wrath.

"Madame, I see your hand in this. You have taught my niece to disobey."

"No, no, Your Majesty! I do not know why you are angry with me!"

But François, losing all control, now shouted at Aymée as Jeanne squirmed under her bedcovers.

"That's enough! Be quiet, woman! Heads will fall for this!"

Aymée blanched and fidgeted with the folds of her green satin dress.

"Oh, Your Majesty! Please explain why you are angry with me."

"Because you have advised my niece to refuse to marry the Duke of Clèves!"

"Never in the world have I done that! What I advised her to do was to obey all the wishes of Your Majesty and of the king her father and of the queen her mother. Ask Jeanne if I have ever advised her otherwise."

"Yes, quite right, Madame. And that is how it should be."

Still agitated, François sat down again, but then abruptly got up and left Jeanne's room.

The king left Plessis that day without coming back to see his niece. But she did have another visitor. The Cardinal de Tournon arrived at the château only a few hours after the king's departure. He brusquely ordered Aymée to let him speak with Jeanne. Aymée, who had experienced a most trying day, meekly obeyed and ushered him into the sick room. The cardinal, resplendent in rich attire, did not waste words on small talk.

"The king has sent me to have a word with you," he said as he stood by the bed, wagging a thick and bejeweled finger, "and he is most displeased with you, child."

Jeanne did not answer but stared at his red robe rebelliously.

"You must comply, child."

The cardinal smiled pompously, sure that his presence would instill fear and shame in Jeanne and a desire to please those older and wiser than herself.

"I would rather die . . ." Jeanne began, almost choking on her words before she continued, "I would rather die than marry the duke."

The cardinal was so shocked that he sat down. Silent for a moment, he contemplated the room. Fine tapestries covered roughcast walls, and where there were no tapestries, rich paneling ornamented with scrollwork sheathed the sides. In the scrollwork the arms of France had been cunningly wrought and the Latin words *Franciscus Francorum Rex,* François, King of the French, had been written. The words fortified his determination to have Jeanne obey.

"If you continue in this disobedience to the king, he will shut you up in a tower."

He then turned to Aymée.

"And as for you, Madame, and for other disobedient ones in your household, let it be known that the penalty will be death. Do you understand?"

Speechless, it was all Aymée could do to nod. She was terrified. But Jeanne was not intimidated. Somewhere outside an owl hooted through the rain, and she recalled what Monsieur Perault had said. It would be clear weather soon. She smiled. Cardinal de Tournon, seeing the smile and thinking it meant submission, smiled as well.

"I would rather kill myself than consent, Monsieur le Cardinal."

After she had said this, she pushed her face under the covers.

The cardinal stood up again, his smile turned to a frown. Not able to fix Jeanne with his stern gaze any longer, he now focused on Aymée.

"I am warning you as a friend. If you cannot make the princess acquiesce to this marriage, it will go badly for you and your household."

Trembling, Aymée drew herself up to her full height. With nervous dignity she said, "His Majesty must do as he thinks fit, but it is not my fault that the princess will not marry the duke. I did not advise her to refuse. But I have always heard her say that she did not want to marry him."

The cardinal, like the king before him, left in a huff. The servants grouped about in the hall and in the kitchen, talking excitedly. They had heard the king shouting and the princess sobbing. Opinions ran two ways. Some thought the princess should never give in, while others thought it would be folly to hold out against the king. Yvette was much sought after in the kitchen, but she remained tight-lipped. All she would say was that the princess, their own dear princess, was much distraught and needed quiet.

12

Hope

In the weeks that followed Jeanne constantly gazed out of the windows into the Plessis forest, hoping desperately that her father would come and rescue her. She hardly noticed the beauty of the long summer evenings, or the scent of the flowers drifting up from the garden. Yvette put bouquets of gillyflowers, cornflowers, and daisies in vases about her room, but Jeanne could not be made to admire them.

"He will come," she told Yvette in a determined voice, "my father will come."

Yvette only nodded. There was nothing she could say, and she was well aware, as were all the servants, that a great many preparations were being made for the wedding. Gently patting Jeanne's shoulder, she led her to the window. Butterflies, in all their bright and patterned flights, danced about from flower to flower.

"Monsieur Perault wonders if you would care to go riding."

"No, I will stay here and watch the lane. Then I will be the first to see . . . to see . . ."

Jeanne's voice trailed off. Tears welled up in her eyes, and she turned away, choosing to mope about on the pillows by the hearth.

A moment later Yvette called out, "Madame Jeanne! Madame Jeanne! Horses are coming, and I do believe they bear the livery of Navarre!"

Jeanne jumped up. Her pulse raced and her mouth felt dry.

"Yes, it is the Navarre coach," Yvette cried as she hugged Jeanne.

Together they stood as six armed horsemen, followed by the coach, made their way across the courtyard. The sharp pain that her parents had put the king's will above her happiness subsided somewhat in Jeanne's heart. She had known all along that her father would come to help her. After all, she was his own flesh and blood.

But the royal party from Navarre was not her father but her mother. And her mother made it very clear, even at the first embrace, she had come only to try and persuade Jeanne that the marriage must take place, and that the king of France must not be trifled with. Every day she repeated the same words, over and again.

"He must be obeyed, Jeanne. He is your king. It should be joy to you to do as he asks."

But every word which Marguerite or Aymée spoke only made the girl more stubborn.

"The king does not think of me, he thinks only of himself. I wish to stay in France. I do not want to go to Clèves. I will not marry the duke. I want . . ."

She stopped. Indeed, she did not know exactly what it was she wanted. But, her mouth quivering, she steadfastly refused to agree. Her mother gently laid a hand on her arm one more time.

"It is a good marriage, Jeanne. Believe me, it is a good marriage. And William is of the Reformed faith."

"I would not care if he was a monkey and had no faith but a banana. I do not want to marry him!"

"Jeanne!" Her mother spoke quietly and reproachfully. But Jeanne was not finished.

"And I suppose you will say next that my marriage with the Duke of Clèves will be as happy as was your first marriage to the Duke of Alençon!"

Marguerite stood up and turned her back on her daughter.

"If you will not obey, you will be beaten."

"You would beat me?"

Disbelief registered in Jeanne's voice. Marguerite did not answer but only indicated with a nod of her head that she would. Still Jeanne refused to yield, and the next few days she was whipped consistently under the supervision of Aymée who wept while the girl was held down. Bruised and humiliated, the twelve-year-old finally consented to the marriage.

The wedding took place at Châtellerault some thirty kilometers south of Plessis-Les-Tours. On June 13, 1541, King François and his entire court, as well as Jeanne and her parents, arrived at the large château. A huge pavilion had been built in front of the main entrance. Crystal chandeliers had been hung in it and thick tapestries adorned its sides. The arms of Valois, Albret, and Clèves were emblazoned all around the courtyard. Tables in and around the pavilion overflowed with food, and singing and dancing went on far into the night. The king had designated the evening as a betrothal celebration, and during the height of the festivities he escorted Jeanne together with the Duke of Clèves to the Cardinal de Tournon.

"Are you, William de la Marck, Duke of Clèves, willing to marry Jeanne, Princess of Navarre?"

"Ja, I am," he replied in a thick guttural accent.

The cardinal then turned to Jeanne. There was somewhat of a triumphant note in his voice as he spoke to the girl who had defied him only weeks before.

"And are you, Jeanne, Princess of Navarre, willing to marry William de la Marck, Duke of Clèves?"

Jeanne did not answer but doggedly stared at the cardinal. He repeated the question two more times, but all she did was smile at him rather tremulously.

"*Ne me pressez point*," she finally spoke out. "Do not press me."

Nothing the cardinal said could induce her to say more.

Later that night, in the privacy of her own apartment at Châtellerault, Jeanne wrote up another protest.

I, Jeanne of Navarre, continue my protests. The marriage between me and the Duke of Clèves is against my will. Anything that I may say or do after this will have been because of force . . . out of fear of my father the king, and of the queen, my mother, who had me threatened and beaten by the Baillive de Caen, my governess. She has several times brought pressure on me at the command of the queen, threatening that if I did not do everything the king wished I would be so beaten and maltreated that I would die, and that I would be the cause of the ruin and destruction of my mother and father and of their house. Therefore I became so frightened and afraid that I did not know to whom to appeal except to God, for I see that my mother and father have abandoned me. They know full well that I will never love the Duke of Clèves and that I do not want anything to do with him. Therefore, I am protesting anew, that, if it should happen that I should be betrothed or married to the said duke . . . in whatever manner it might come about, it will have been against my desire, that he will never be my husband, that I will never consider him so, and that the marriage will be null and void. I call on God and on you as my witnesses, and ask that you sign with me and show that you know the force, violence, and constraint that have been used against me to make me enter the said marriage.

Jeanne's doctor, Francesque Navarro, together with a servant, witnessed the protest. But the girl knew, even as she watched the two men sign, that there was no escape. She must marry the duke in the morning, and no miracle would prevent it.

13

THE WEDDING

The beatings had ceased weeks ago when Jeanne had finally agreed to the marriage. Nevertheless, her body was still bruised as she was dressed for her wedding, and she winced as attendants pulled her gown over her head. The morning dawned bright and sunny, and Jeanne's beloved birds sang their feathered hearts out in the trees around Châtellerault. All the women agreed that the singing and the sunshine were good omens, which meant that the princess would surely have many, many years of happiness with the duke. Jeanne did not speak. She had not slept well and was tired.

"Look," Aymée exclaimed as she glanced down into the courtyard below, "I can see the ambassadors from Portugal, Venice, and Saxony passing beneath. They have come from all over the world to see you wed, Jeanne."

But Jeanne neither responded nor looked at her governess. All too well she recalled the beatings and how Aymée had given her consent to them.

A golden circlet was placed on Jeanne's shining brown hair. A cloak of crimson satin with an edging of ermine was draped over a gold and silver skirt trimmed with precious stones. The ladies clapped their hands in delight over the picture the young girl made, and, indeed, she looked like a fairy-tale princess. But Jeanne did not feel like a fairy-tale princess. She seemed, in her own mind, to be taking part in some great play. Glittering, she walked down the great stairs of the château toward the pavilion. Her attendants trailed behind; her parents walked by her side; and her right hand limply lay in that of her mother's. The cloth of gold about her waist cascaded down to below her ankles. It was so heavy with jewels that each step was slow and cumbersome. All around people oohed and ahhed.

The duke stepped forward to greet her as she entered the pavilion. He bowed before his bride and held out a diamond ring. The buckles on his shoes, as well as the diamond in his hand, caught the sunlight.

"*Mein liebes Mädchen*," he murmered, "My sweet girl."

She understood the words and blushed slightly. Mutely she stretched out her hand, and William slid the precious ring onto her finger. An altar now stood where there had been singing and dancing the night before. Covered with a cloth of gold, it bore the arms of both the duke and the princess. It was just before noon, and the air was so bright that the roof of the canopied pavilion shimmered.

Something gave way in Jeanne's heart. She glanced at the tall, young man who had walked on to take his place at the front, and fervently wished for the hundredth time that day that she were a bird so that she could fly to the top of the tent and watch all the people below without touching them. The duke was to be her husband, and she did not know him! Fearing and rebelling simultaneously, she suddenly refused to move.

The entire procession had halted when William greeted his bride. It was a tender moment and everyone was indulgent. But when Jeanne did not follow her groom to the front to stand beside him under the canopy and continued to stand still for more than two minutes, the delay grew uncomfortable. Everyone—Jeanne's attendants, her parents, the king, the multitude of ambassadors, the constable of France, the dauphin, and many more—waited for her to move. Jeanne knew many of them, and yet she knew none of them. Who were they to her and she to them? For a moment she longed fiercely for Toinette and for the comfort of her arms. As if she were rooted to the spot, Jeanne remained where she was.

"Move, girl!" Marguerite who was still standing next to her, hissed the words into her ear.

The king frowned and, leaving his gentlemen, came toward them. Marguerite stepped aside to make room for her brother. François was resplendent in a white satin doublet decorated with pearls and emeralds. Without any ceremony, he took Jeanne's arm and pinched. There was no doubt that he was angry, but he was unable to vent his fury before such a large crowd. His fingers pinched again, and tears welled up in her eyes. But still she did not budge. The great weight of her gown made her a solid object, and the king, for fear of appearing ridiculous, did not pull.

"I cannot walk," she whispered, and only the king heard her, "I am unwell, and the dress—the dress is too heavy."

The king took in the assembly of gawking wedding participants. Inwardly fuming, he motioned for the constable of France, Montmorency, to approach. Everyone knew François had no great liking for Montmorency, a staunch Roman Catholic and a man who was becoming increasingly powerful.

Montmorency had, in times past, criticized Marguerite, especially with regard to her tolerance and protection of the new religion. The ambassadors, courtiers, ladies, and gentlemen of the court all craned their necks to see what would happen.

"Lift the princess," the king commanded the constable who had dutifully come forward, "and carry her to the altar!"

Montmorency stiffened. This was a humbling assignment. His job as constable was to protect France, to fight battles. It was not to carry girls to the altar. He hesitated for a moment, a big man, a soldier, thoroughly humiliated by the king's command. But he dared not refuse. Nodding curtly, he stooped over, swinging a mighty arm under Jeanne's great golden skirt. She put both arms around his neck and closed her eyes. There was no helping it. History would march on, as Monsieur de Bourbon always said. And here she was, marching on toward the altar carried by one of France's greatest soldiers.

Montmorency deposited Jeanne rather rudely onto the space under the velvet canopy by the altar. She stayed where he put her, her arms held stiffly at her side. William glanced at her anxiously, but she remained frozen as the Nuptial Mass was played. The group of musicians at the side of the pavilion outdid themselves in harmony. It was a melodious piece for violas, flutes, pipes, and lute, and had she not been so upset, Jeanne would have gloried in the sound of it. The ensuing ceremony was a blur in Jeanne's mind, and she shrank from its reality.

After the ceremony, William's herald cried out, *Largesse*, and threw many gold and silver coins into the crowd of people from the surrounding countryside. Amid their cheers and applause, Jeanne could not help but think that her misery was making other people glad.

Dinner was served in the great hall of the château. No money had been spared. King François had been generous for he greatly desired this marriage, this alliance that would bind the Duchy of Clèves to France. There were two long head tables. Jeanne and William sat at the center of one while François sat at the center of the other. The hall was hung with cloths of gold and magnificent vases of silver were displayed on a side table. The vases were a gift to the bridal couple from François. Jeanne ate almost nothing. William said very little. His command of the French language was limited. But he smiled at Jeanne from time to time, offering her tidbits of food.

"Ich lege dir ein kleines stüchen fleisch auf deinen teller" — "I put a little piece of meat on your plate."

His voice was low and apologetic, and she felt sorry for him, for it seemed he was trying to please her. Politely she smiled but pushed the meat to the edge of her plate without eating it. After the dinner, there was dancing and a masquerade.

While everyone was still making merry and laughing, the ladies-in-waiting took Jeanne back to her bedchamber. Gently undressing her, they clothed her in a white shift made of silk. Brown hair flowed down her thin shoulders and past her tiny waist. Jeanne alternately shivered and sighed. Through the window she could hear the piping sound of the musicians playing and the laughter of the guests. Aymée clapped her hands, and the women stopped their chattering.

"It is time, ma petite," Aymée said softly, "to go to the marriage chamber, where the king himself will see you bedded down. Don't worry," she added, seeing the whiteness of Jeanne's face, "remember, it is only a ceremony."

The first thing Jeanne saw upon entering the nuptial chamber was a huge bed with an extravagant canopy. Cautiously she walked toward it. Surely she would disappear into that bed, and no one would ever find her again. Aymée, together with the ladies, helped Jeanne climb in. They covered her with a soft, white linen sheet, and then discreetly stepped back. A few minutes later, out of the corner of her eye, Jeanne saw William and his attending gentlemen enter through the great oak doorway. King François, her father, her mother, and all the greatest lords and ladies of the court, followed him. She pulled the coverlet tightly about herself and flushed. No one spoke. William looked slightly ill at ease but then, prodded by King François, strode toward her. Smilingly he lifted his right foot and sank a large boot onto the feather bed. The dark leather looked rough and out of place against the smoothness of the sheets, and the weight of his foot made Jeanne slide a bit to the left. In spite of herself, she looked William in the eye. He winked at her, and she turned beet-red. Then he took his foot off the bed and walked back to take his place within the assembled group of his gentlemen. King François walked to the center of the room. Turning about, he spoke to everyone who was assembled.

"Ladies and gentlemen, this marriage has now been sufficiently celebrated, for we consider the bride too young to further share her husband's bed as yet. But let it be remembered by everyone that they are husband and wife. Let it be remembered that this is a binding marriage."

At this point he looked over his shoulder to glance sharply at Jeanne under the covers. Then he shouted out to the whole assembly, "Long live the Duke and Duchess of Clèves."

The festivities lasted a full week, and then William returned to Clèves. Charles V was seriously threatening the little duchy, and there were many German battles to fight and properties for him to defend. Meanwhile, Jeanne, the child bride, the little Duchess of Clèves, was shipped back to Plessis-Les-Tours to continue her education.

14
MEMORIES

It was the opinion of Yvette, and she was quick to share it once they were back at Tours, that Jeanne's mother had given in with regard to the marriage only on the condition that it be one in name only.

"And your father," Yvette said, as she warmed Jeanne's rail in front of the fireplace before helping her into it, "your father never consented to the marriage. He only endured it. I saw it on his face. He did not want to anger the king."

"I was afraid," Jeanne replied slowly as she gazed into the flames, "I was truly afraid that I would die if I did not marry the duke."

Yvette patted her on the shoulder.

"I know," she said, "I know."

She padded over to the dresser, picked up a silver-plated brush and stood behind Jeanne, who sat in a small, straight-back chair in front of the hearth. Slowly and rhythmically she began her strokes.

"But I did protest," Jeanne stood up so suddenly that Yvette's brush tangled, "I did protest, and the Estates of Béarn, which my father governs and which I will someday govern, objected to the marriage also, because they did not want me, their future ruler, to live in the Germanies, in far-away Cléves."

"I hear that Germany," Yvette whispered in a low voice as she carefully retrieved the brush dangling in Jeanne's long hair, "is a rather crude and uncivilized country. Our princess will do well to stay here, I think."

Jeanne smiled at her rather wistfully. It was what she herself hoped.

The year passed slowly from summer to fall to winter. Jeanne often felt unwell and had no appetite, and even her beloved green parrot failed to make her smile. It seemed that marriage, even if only in name, did not agree with her. Marguerite, a faithful mother-in-law, wrote to William.

Dear Monsieur de Clèves, my son:

Jeanne is well but still very thin, and for two months has been poorly. We are doing everything to fatten her up, but she does not gain weight. She should be better now, because winter agrees with her better than summer. I am concerned for her health because I wish her soon to be able to be with you. She has had, this November, a serious spell of vomiting blood, but did recover.

The king wants Jeanne to go to Fontainebleau, but twice she has fallen very ill there; it is such a damp place. I await the time, devoutly wished for, when I can send her to you, but only God can give her health and strength, which I pray he may give you also.

As they were sitting together one evening, Aymée told Jeanne that her mother and father were expecting another child.

"Your mother is very happy about it," the governess said, studying Jeanne's youthful profile as she sat in front of the fire.

Jeanne digested the information and ran a long, white finger down the satin of her soft blue skirt. It seemed so far removed from her—a baby brother or sister. Then she frowned.

"If it is a boy, they will be very happy."

"Hush," Aymée said, "the child is not yet born, and your mother is, well, she is not as young as she used to be. Bearing children is not easy."

"You think there is danger?"

The flames in the hearth danced to the quickening of Jeanne's heartbeat. She had not forgiven her mother for forcing her into marriage with William, but she did not wish her ill.

"We always need God's protection, Jeanne, but especially so when . . ."

Aymée stopped in mid-sentence, and Jeanne was silent, thinking about the little brother who had been born about two years after herself. He had not lived very long. She vaguely remembered that her mother had paid a visit to Lonray at the time of his death; she vaguely recalled as well that her mother had wept a lot.

"Tell me about when I was born, Aymée."

Her governess wrinkled her forehead.

"That's a long time ago, Jeanne."

"You were there, were you not?"

"Yes, I was."

"Well, tell me then whatever you remember."

Aymée closed her eyes. With clarity she saw the room in which Jeanne had been born, and with even greater clarity she saw Marguerite as she had walked the floor of the apartment on her mother's arm. Louise of Savoy had been healthy then. Ramrod straight, the woman had encouraged her daughter to keep on walking, had told her to ignore the work her body was doing in bringing forth a child, an heir.

"No, Maman," Marguerite had said, "not an heir, but an heiress. Even though I wish for a boy, I know it will be a girl."

She had been right. Marguerite was usually right. And here was the heiress sitting right in front of her, asking about her birth.

"Don't brood so, Aymée." Jeanne's voice interrupted her thoughts. "You must remember something you can tell me."

"It was a very cold day," Aymée began, "and icy rain and snow fell at the same time, and the sky was dark. It was November, and winter had set in early. There were fires in all the great rooms of the palace at Nérac."

"Which room was I born in?"

Jeanne's voice was eager. She knew the palace well. Although she did not visit it often, she explored when she did.

"It was the room at the far end of the east wing—a room of which your mother was very fond."

"Was Maman excited about my birth? Was Papa there?"

Aymée was quiet again for a bit before she spoke. She knew she must choose her words carefully. The truth was that Marguerite had called again and again for her brother and had not once asked for her husband. Even now, some fifteen years later, it was easy to hear Marguerite's petulant voice.

"I cannot believe," she had said, "that the child will presume to be born without my brother the king's presence and command."

"Well," Jeanne's impatient voice interrupted again, "what is it you are thinking, Aymée and what is it you recall?"

"I recall that . . . that you were born around five o'clock in the afternoon, and that all the citizens of Nérac prayed for your safe delivery."

"All of them?"

"Yes, I do believe that all of them did."

"Why?"

"Because your grandmother had sent a messenger into town saying that there was some danger and that you were slow in coming, keeping both the doctor and your mother waiting."

"I was slow?"

Jeanne grinned now. She thought it quite funny that she had kept her mother waiting.

"But you made up for your slowness in lung power. When you were finally born, you cried so loudly it almost broke the chandelier on the ceiling."

Jeanne laughed out loud. "Did I?"

"Yes, and then you were baptized."

"I thought I was baptized in the cathedral?"

"You were baptized in the cathedral. But your father insisted that you also be baptized immediately. A priest came, I believe his name was Father Roudry, and he sprinkled you with water right there in the bedroom. 'And though a child be but half-born, head and neck and no more, do not hesitate.

Christen it and cast it on the water.' Those were the words he read from his manual."

"Was I . . . was I a nice-looking baby?"

"You were beautiful, Jeanne. Your eyes were so large—they looked out at everyone and everything so steadily that it was remarked you would undoubtedly be very smart."

"Did Maman think so too?" Jeanne asked wistfully.

Aymée lost no time in assuring her.

"She did think so. And you know who else thought so? All the people of Nérac."

"Why do you say so? Did Maman allow them all into the bedchamber to peek at me?"

"No, you silly goose, of course not. But at the public baptism a few months later the road to the cathedral was lined with crowds of people. A very colorful group of people as I remember."

"What sort of people? Why do you say colorful?"

"Well, there were merchants who wore red robes, and archers and crossbowmen from Nérac in their uniforms, grocers in green damask, goldsmiths in blue satin, and haberdashers in brown satin. And all the women and children had gathered blossoms. What a sight—and the noise! All the bells in the district were peeling, Jeanne, loudly and merrily because of the great rejoicing in your baptism that day."

"Was Uncle François there as well?"

"To be sure. Your father and mother went down the road first in their carriage. The people cheered for them. Then your Uncle François rode by on his horse. He was a sight to see, your uncle. Clothed in purple velvet, he rode a horse richly caparisoned. A hundred or so foot soldiers marched in front and behind him. But the people had no eyes for his pomp and quietly moved aside to let him pass. Then we came, you and I, Jeanne, in another carriage. It was upholstered in red velvet. I remember because it was so soft to sit on. I held you on my lap, and, baby though you were, you were dressed magnificently. A little crimson mantle hung over your tiny shoulders. It had a train furred with ermine and was fastened about your throat. And your gown was all lace and jewels, with long hanging sleeves. You could barely sit up in the ceremonial robes but you should have heard the shouting as we passed. The people could hardly contain themselves for you have always been their special princess and they have always loved you."

"The love of those you do not know is . . ." Jeanne hesitated, picking her words slowly. "Well, it is not as sweet as the love of those whom you do know."

Aymée did not respond to this but went on with her story.

"Inside the Cathedral the Cardinal de Bourbon waited to baptize you. You were a naked little bundle there at the baptismal font, Jeanne, and you squalled so loudly the windows shook. I recall how the cardinal frowned and looked at me. As if I could make you stop screaming. And all the people smiled at the noise you were making."

Jeanne smiled as well. It was a good story after all, and she was in it.

"And then?" she asked.

"Well, as quickly as I could, I redressed you in all your finery. Then the cardinal anointed you with holy oil. It dribbled down your tiny forehead and onto your cheeks. But you seemed not to mind and began to coo. It echoed and reechoed off the walls in the church. Both your father and your uncle smiled at the same time."

"No doubt," Jeanne said, "they were thinking of the time when they could marry me off to some rich prince who would be of benefit to them."

Aymée clucked her tongue in disapproval. "You mustn't always think the worst," she said, "and you must remember that your mother and father do love you."

Now it was Jeanne's turn to cluck her tongue. But at the same time she hoped that her mother, who was well in her forties, would come through this new birthing safely.

15

THE ANNULMENT

In the spring of 1543, Marguerite bore twins. They did not live long, and two little coffins were carried in quick succession to the grave. Jeanne pondered much on this. Why were babies born if only to die? The conversation she'd had with Aymée was still fresh in her mind. Had she lived because there was a divine purpose for her life? And what was this purpose?

One day as she and the master of the stables were out riding, Jeanne said, "You've told me often, Monsieur Perault, that birds predict the weather. Do you think that birds worship as Catholics or as Protestants?"

Startled at the question, Monsieur Perault stared at Jeanne, but saw that she was serious.

"All God's creatures worship him in their own manner, Madame Princess," he said.

"You are a creature, Monsieur Perault," she rejoined. "How do you worship?"

He was silent. She nudged her horse closer to his and laid a hand on his reins.

"You must not fear me, Monsieur Perault," she softly said.

"Well," Monsieur Perault spoke softly as well, "I have seen the Catholic processions on holy days in Paris, as I know you have also seen. I have watched endless parades of relics—dead bones in gold boxes. Barefooted priests carrying gold crosses and red-robed bishops with no smiles and all the time bells tolling and drums rolling so that the pavement trembled."

"Yes," she prodded.

"And," he continued, stroking his horse's mane, "I have not seen God in it."

Jeanne was silent a moment before she ventured more.

"Then you do not pray to the saints?"

"No," Monsieur Perault answered. He seemed to want to say more but was prevented by a shout from one of the groomsmen a few feet behind them.

"A rider approaches—a rider wearing royal livery."

The rider was a messenger from King François. His horse, flecked with foam, trotted up alongside Jeanne and Monsieur Perault.

"Madame, the king bids me tell you that your husband, the Duke of Clèves, has lost all his forces to Charles V. Not only that, but he has totally surrendered the Duchy of Clèves to Charles, renounced his alliance with France, and has returned to the Catholic faith. Your uncle, his royal majesty, King François, therefore," the messenger went on, hot and sweaty from riding hard and fast, "requests your presence at Alençon."

Never quite comfortable at being summoned to court, Jeanne was in no hurry to obey her uncle's request. Besides that, the weather was unpleasant that fall of 1544. Late September rain made travel especially undesirable, leaving the roads rutted with huge potholes. But together with Aymée and several of her attending ladies, Jeanne set out for Alençon a few days later. The ground was so soft that the horses made poor time, their hooves sometimes sinking into the mud up to their fetlocks.

As she looked out at the dreary landscape through the carriage window, Jeanne pondered her marriage to William. She had respectfully written to him from time to time, prodded by Aymée as well as her mother, but she had felt little, if any, affection for him. Would Uncle François now send her to Clèves? She was, after all, almost sixteen now and quite grownup. As the carriage swayed from side to side and as the rain pelted on the roof, she voiced her fears to Aymée.

"The king determined to give me to William without listening to me, and when I tried to speak to my mother, she would not listen either but pressured me to marry. Do you think that Uncle François will send me to Germany, Aymée?"

Aymée did not answer but lurched forward as the carriage hit a bump. Jeanne continued as if speaking to herself.

"I was abandoned by everyone and so turned to God. He was my only recourse. God has now granted me the blessing that the Duke of Clèves has committed crimes that possibly relieve the king and my father and mother of the necessity of sending me to Germany. They would not send me there now, would they?"

The question ended in a wail.

After staring out the window for a few minutes, she turned back to Aymée, nudging her with a despairing little gesture.

"Will they listen to me now?"

Many servants were lined up in the pouring rain as the princess alighted from her carriage. Weary, with both travel and worry, Jeanne was relieved that her uncle was not on hand to greet her. She had heard that he had been ill of late. Taken to her apartments, warmed by some hot ale, and dressed in a comfortable, woolen shift embroidered with roses, she almost fell asleep before King François finally sent for her.

"Your Majesty." Jeanne bowed and kissed the extended hand, noting at once how blue the veins were and how the hand trembled.

"Niece."

It was not a strong voice. As a matter of fact, it bore no resemblance at all to the voice that had shouted at her when she, ill in bed, had refused to marry William. She lifted her face and studied her uncle. Rather hunched up, he seemed lost in his chair and uncharacteristically frail.

"Uncle?"

He coughed and motioned for some papers to be handed to him.

"You know, do you not, Jeanne," François spoke slowly, sitting up straight as he did so, "that you are wedded to a traitor—a traitor to France!"

Jeanne shifted her feet and was, at first, at a loss to answer. But then her common sense and a feeling of anger took over. "If I am, it is because you made me marry him."

The king laughed weakly.

"You are no diplomat, child. I fear such an answer will not do at all."

She made no response, but her face was set, and she could not bring herself to smile at him. Unperturbed, François continued.

"Come, come, Jeanne. I know you were married for reasons of state, but such is the way with royalty. The truth is that

I will not allow you to remain married to a traitor to France. Well, there it is, and I hope you are not overly bothered. We shall see to it that the pope will grant you an annulment."

"An annulment?"

"Yes, an annulment. You will be free, child. Free as a bird, and you will not have to leave us to go to some faraway place."

Jeanne did not answer her uncle. She might be given freedom for a while, she thought, but sooner or later this freedom, like a captive bird's wings, would be clipped.

A few months later at the Cathedral of Tours, immediately after Mass, Jeanne was called to stand before several bishops. In a clear voice, she read from a paper in her hand:

> I swear and affirm that I do not now and never have felt myself bound or obligated to the said Sieur de Clèves in lawful marriage nor do I wish to take him as my husband. I swear that what was done at the time of the pretended betrothal and ceremony was done in the way described in my protests. I ask that the notaries who are present take note of this declaration.

When she finished, one of the bishops handed Jeanne a Bible. She placed her hand on its cover and vowed she had told the truth.

On October 12, 1545, Pope Paul III dissolved the Clèves marriage on the grounds that Jeanne had consented only because of violence applied, that she had protested, and that the marriage had been one in name only. At the age of almost seventeen, Jeanne was now a single princess once more.

16

The Death of the King

"The king of England has died."

It had been about a year and a half since Jeanne's annulment, and she continued to live at Plessis. Yvette, who always seemed to be the first to hear news about and around Plessis, Paris, and any other place, gave Jeanne the information as she woke her one morning.

"Henry VIII is dead?"

Jeanne yawned, stretching her arms above her head as she repeated Yvette's words. The girl nodded.

"They say too many wives and the gout killed him."

"Who says?"

Yvette shrugged.

"Everyone. That's who. Well, when you marry six wives and behead the lot of them—"

"Yvette," Jeanne laughed as she interrupted the girl, "he didn't behead all of them. He divorced the first one, the third one died in childbed, and the last one is still living. And Anne of Clèves, who would have been my sister-in-law," here she made a face, "why that lady's marriage to Henry was annulled, as was mine."

"Well," Yvette grumbled as she brought Jeanne's stockings to the bed, "all I can say is that he's dead now. As dead as we'll all be sooner or later, I reckon, whether we're kings or not."

"My uncle, the king of France, will not take the news well. They were of the same age and of the same constitution. He will think of Henry's death as . . ." She stopped for a moment, groping for words, before adding softly, ". . . as his own death, I think."

Jeanne had spoken pensively and thought of François who had been ill off and on now for some three years. She'd not seen him during her last visit to court, but all the rumor was that he was not long for this world. Yet in spite of his ill health, he still hunted in the forest around Fontainebleau, as well as in other forests. No longer able to stay on horseback, he had himself carried after the hounds on a stretcher. It was reported that he had said, "After I'm dead, I shall continue to hunt in my coffin."

Jeanne shuddered as she sat on the edge of her bed. What a gloomy thing to think about on such a beautiful day. Yvette, on her knees in front of the bed, drew a green silk cord through the green silk eyelet holes on the bottom of Jeanne's left stocking, tying it off at the top with a clock. The sun shone through the grille on the window, making light bars on the floor. Jeanne poked a stockinged toe at the dust particles dancing in front of the bed.

Even though she had not seen Uncle François when she visited Fontainebleau a few months ago, she had seen someone else. She had seen Antoine de Bourbon, Duke of Vendôme. The elder of the Bourbon princes, he was as royal as the Valois family, and first Prince of the Blood. He had sat next to her at one of the banquets—a banquet that had been given to celebrate the birthday of Catherine de Medicis, the wife of her cousin Henri who was first heir to the throne. Antoine had been very attentive. He had kissed her hand and had said that she was pretty. He had often sought her out, and she had walked with him in the garden. She had even allowed him to kiss her. She smiled to herself. Yvette was quick to pick up on it.

"You'll not be smiling because the English king's dead?"

But Jeanne could not be coaxed into confidences. She simply swung her feet contentedly as Yvette busied herself with shaking out a light gown, a gown the color of sunlight.

"This dress," she said, "will match your mood."

Two months later word arrived at Plessis that King François had also died. Aymée and Jeanne received the young messenger, one Jacques Montain, in the *grande salle*. After being provided with cider and warmth, he told them what had happened.

"His Majesty, the king, your uncle, was not content to stay in one place. The court moved about at his whims, traveling at great speed from one château to another. We were all amazed at his power of endurance because he had incessant pain by day and his nights were very bad."

Aymée laid a finger on her lips. She did not think this good for Jeanne to hear. But Jeanne prodded the man on.

"Were you there when my uncle died, Jacques Montain?"

"Well, we were at the château at Loches. Your uncle wanted to celebrate Mardi Gras there. But his pain became so bad that he did not stay. Instead, he left for Saint-Germain to see his court physician, Ambroise Paré. He stopped overnight at Rambouillet and, in a last burst of strength, took part in the hunt there. Then he took to his bed and could not be moved."

Aymée again motioned with her head, trying to get Jacques to stop. But Jeanne wanted to know the details.

"Go on, Jacques," she said.

Jacques took another drink of the cider, wiped his mouth, and continued.

"Well, the confessor was sent for, and His Majesty, your uncle, made confession. You can be easy in your mind about that. But he was not easy in his mind himself. We were in the hall, many of us, just standing about, waiting. And we could hear your uncle, God rest his soul, crying out and weeping.

" 'The stakes,' " he cried out, " 'I can see them burning. I can hear the voices.' "

"The Waldensians," Jeanne murmured, thinking of the hundreds of people slaughtered by her uncle some three years ago . . . simply because they read the Bible and refused to acknowledge the pope.

Jacques had stopped talking and seemed rather embarrassed by his own frankness. The late king was, after all, the princess's uncle, and she must feel some pain about the way in which he died. But Jeanne motioned that he should keep talking.

"I was not in the room, not with him, you understand. But I have heard others say that he asked for the story of Mary Magdalene and that his confessor read it to him before administering extreme unction. Yet even then, I have heard, he was not at ease."

"Was my mother . . ." Jeanne asked, "was her Majesty, the queen of Navarre, present?"

"No, Her Majesty, your mother, was resting at a convent in Poitou. But she has been sent word."

"She will take it hard," Jeanne said as if to herself, and then, turning back to Jacques, "What then? What happened then?"

"Last to be summoned to the king's bedside was your royal cousin, the dauphin, Prince Henri. Henri asked for his father's blessing, and it is said that he swooned upon the bed. It is also said that your uncle held him, but because of his weakness was unable to release him."

Jeanne sighed. She remembered the splendor of François who had always been decked out in fine clothes, who had smelled like musk, and who had towered in both rage and laughter. Fine clothes then, as well as grooming and physical appearance, meant nothing, nothing at all. The spirit of the body must always return to God who had given it.

"You may go," Jeanne said.

She waved her small hand at the man. He stood up, bowed, and took his leave. Aymée moved closer to the fire, shivering even though it was warm in the room.

"Perhaps," she said, "you should now consider traveling back to Nérac, your birthplace. With your uncle, the king of France, gone, guardianship will revert back to your parents, the king and queen of Navarre."

"Perhaps," Jeanne agreed as she stood up to retire for the night.

Later, as she lay in bed, it was not her uncle of whom she thought, but Antoine de Bourbon. She imagined him, with the other members of her uncle's household, following the prescribed ritual of casting broken scepters into the grave, as the herald cried, "King François is no more. Long live our gracious sovereign Henri II, whom God preserve."

17

A Second Betrothal

In July 1547, three months after the death of her uncle, Jeanne traveled with her father to Rheims in northeastern France for the coronation of Henri II. On the day of the crowning, attended by her ladies and intensely curious as to whether or not she would see Antoine, Jeanne took much greater care with her clothes than she usually did.

It was a warm day and reminded Jeanne of her wedding day to the Duke of Clèves. The birds had sung on that day as well, but surely today they caroled better. For was she not a single maid once more, and might she not see Antoine as he attended the king?

Yvette, ever able to read Jeanne's moods, teased her. "Will you cover your hair under a coif, or shall I comb it out so that it falls out like a chestnut mantle on your back? Will you wear the black of mourning or your fine red gown? Madame, your mother, still mourns your uncle in the monastery and perhaps . . ."

She stopped and Jeanne laughed.

"Stop your teasing, Yvette, and call my women in. You know that I shall dress well. All the lords and ladies of the court will be at the coronation today. And—"

She broke off and blushed.

Now it was Yvette's turn to laugh. But then Jeanne wrinkled her high forehead and raised her delicately arched eyebrows. Her gray eyes became somewhat unsure as she posed a question.

"They say Henri asked that his mistress, Diane Poitiers, be permitted to take part in the coronation but that this was refused. Indeed, he does not appear to love his wife, Catherine de Médicis, at all. Not that," she continued pensively, "I blame him, for she seems so cold and so . . . well, so menacing when she looks at you. But she is, after all, his lawfully wedded wife. She must be sad, or perhaps very angry, that Henri ignores her so pointedly."

Yvette shrugged.

"It is the way of court. One marries for politics, and one loves outside of marriage."

Jeanne sat up very straight and retorted angrily.

"I will never do so! I will marry only for love! And now, call the women so that they may dress me."

Later that morning Jeanne joined the huge procession of French nobility gathered for the coronation and together with them trailed Henri into the Cathedral of Rheims. She took her place in that great and magnificent church and watched as her cousin made his way to the front of the Cathedral alone. Ceremonial vestments awaited him on the altar—vestments that had also been worn by his father, François the First, at his coronation. Jeanne heard whispers behind her as she stood in her pew, whispers that said that these were not the original vestments but copies. Not too far from the front, Jeanne had a good view of the altar. She could plainly see that the sky-blue satin tunic Henri wore, sewn with golden fleurs-de-lis and trimmed with crimson, bore an added decoration: a border of pearl embroidery fashioned to spell out the initials D and H.

D for Diane and H for Henri and no C for Catherine. How unfaithful and how wicked! she fumed to herself. *How can he swear fealty to the people of France if he cannot be loyal to his own wife?*

Her eyes flashed in disdain as Henri donned the ceremonial sandals and the great mantle. Her heart beat with anger as he received the sword, scepter, golden spurs, and crown of Charlemagne.

Behind Henri, against the wall and beyond the pomp and ceremony of the moment, hung the cross of Christ. Jeanne fixed her eyes on it. *Did loyalty to others begin with the cross?* she wondered. She knew that Monsieur Cauvin, who still wrote to her mother at regular intervals, would answer "yes." She also knew Monsieur Roussel and others she respected, including Monsieur Perault, would answer "yes" as well. But then her eyes met the eyes of Antoine de Bourbon who stood next to Henri. Her thoughts faltered and her self-examination stopped.

In the spring of the following year, Jeanne was summoned to court for a personal audience with her cousin, the new king. It was with great trepidation that she answered the summons. For what would cousin Henri say? What would he require of her? She was, after all, a princess and, as such, someone to be manipulated—a pawn. Her father, although disabled with an attack of gout and disgruntled with the pain, was not too pleased with what he also supposed would be another marriage suggestion.

"Spain is still possible," he counseled her, "and don't you forget it. I think Henri would like to marry you to the Duke of Guise. But what good would that do Navarre? None! None, at all! Don't forget that you are a Princess of the Blood and that you will be the queen of Navarre someday!"

Jeanne paled at her father's comments. She had hoped that perhaps Henri might ask her to consider Antoine as husband. As a Prince of the Blood, he was also an equal match. Sighing deeply and squaring her shoulders, she steeled herself before going in to meet with her cousin.

Henri stood up in a gesture of deference when Jeanne entered his chamber. His handsome, dark face seemed friendly, and his voice was cordial.

"Well, Cousin," he said, rubbing his hands together, "and how is your father, the king of Navarre?"

Inwardly Jeanne breathed a sigh of relief. Perhaps this interview would not be as difficult as she had imagined.

"Well enough," she answered somewhat shyly, "but he suffers of late from the gout."

"Perhaps," Henri said, "we should send him our surgeon, Ambroise Paré. He is very skilled and might be of some use."

Jeanne inclined her head by way of acknowledging his courtesy.

"Sit down, fair cousin," Henri continued, "for I have a mind to speak frankly and openly with you."

She took her place in a low chair, and he also sat down opposite her. Eyeing his rather large, dominant nose, Jeanne suddenly had an urge to laugh. Surely that nose got in the way when he kissed his Diane. It was nerves she told herself, and bit her lip. But try as she might, she could not keep a smile off her face.

"Why do you smile?"

Henri smiled as well, and Jeanne racked her brain to think of an answer.

"Your Majesty is very kind to me," she ventured, "and this makes me happy."

He did not respond but, after rubbing his face thoughtfully, called an attendant for some mulled wine.

"This wine comes from Chenonceaux. Diane's own vineyards have produced it. I believe you will enjoy it."

Jeanne stiffened perceptibly. She neither liked nor respected Diane Poitiers. Her fingers grasped the goblet he offered her, but she did not drink.

"Cousin," Henri said again, and he drank freely and enthusiastically, wiping his hand across his mouth afterwards, "you are of an age to marry. That is why I have called you here."

Jeanne looked down at her hands and made no response.

"Well," Henri cajoled, "surely you have something to say on the matter. Come, come, little Cousin, don't be shy."

Jeanne looked up, gazing him full in the face. "I have no desire, cousin," she said at length, "to be married again. I think you recall the problems with my first marriage and how—"

He interrupted, putting his goblet down on the small table between them with some force.

"That was no marriage. We both know that was no marriage at all. No, Cousin, the marriage I have in mind for you, you will like much better."

Her gray eyes questioned him, and he continued.

"There are two men, both of the highest rank, who have approached me for your hand. The one is François, the Duke of Guise, and the other is Antoine, the Duke of Vendôme."

At the mention of Antoine, Jeanne's cheeks became pink. She grew warm. Seeing that Henri waited for her to speak, she forced herself to think clearly.

"The Duke of Guise—" she began, but Henri interrupted again, somewhat eagerly.

"I knew you would choose him," he said, "for he is a great prince as well as an excellent soldier."

Jeanne nodded in agreement. She saw it would not be wise to disagree. But she continued slowly and carefully.

"You are right, Your Majesty. The Duke of Guise is a great prince and part of a powerful family. When his niece, Mary of Scotland, marries your son, the Dauphin, his family will grow even more powerful. And if he, through me, becomes king of Navarre also . . ."

Jeanne paused for effect. She wanted her words to sink in before she continued.

"Well, then it seems to me that the Duke of Guise might be equal to Your Majesty in power."

A scowl appeared on Henri's face. He was not a keenly intelligent man, and his ponderous mind delighted in the complete devotion of those around him. He was silent for some time, and Jeanne ventured to continue.

"The Duke of Vendôme is a great prince as well as a brave soldier. I should be honored if you would betroth me to him."

Henri picked up his goblet again. He slowly swirled the wine around and appeared to be considering the matter. At length he nodded.

"Ah, little Cousin," he said, "I think you have made the right choice."

Jeanne inclined her head graciously while inwardly her heart soared. She could barely believe that she had just been given permission to marry the man she loved and one who said that he also loved her.

18

A Second Wedding

It was October 20, 1548, and, as Jeanne told all who surrounded her, the most beautiful day of the whole year, no, of all time. Her ladies laughed as they pulled a golden gown embossed with intricate flower and bird designs over her head. It was Sunday, the first day of the week and surely, Jeanne thought to herself, the first day of true happiness. She walked about carefully but could not help the fact that she began pirouetting. Her feet would do nothing but dance.

"You smile too much," Yvette whispered in her ear.

Jeanne's grin became even more pronounced. She felt so merry that she was about to burst. Surveying her ladies in their bodices of blue satin and skirts of black velvet, bliss overwhelmed her. The gentlemen, she knew, would be clad in black and crimson. What a stately procession they would all make to the church, and what a difference with the time she had been carried up the aisle, wretched and tearful, by Montmorency. At that time she had refused to answer the cardinal's questions no matter how he stared and prodded. But today she would answer—answer clearly and happily. Today she would vow eternal love to Antoine!

The inner courtyard at Moulins, the place of the betrothal and of the wedding, had been transformed into an immense banqueting hall. Music, singing, and laughter resounded throughout the evening, and the hundreds of torches hung on the walls cast cozy shadows. Thousands of candles on the tables flickered steadily, brightening the festivities. It had been a sweet ceremony. Jeanne's voice had exultantly proclaimed to all that she was content.

"I, Jeanne of Navarre, do solemnly promise to take you, Antoine de Bourbon, Duke of Vendôme, as my lawfully wedded husband."

Antoine's voice as well had been firm but also tender as he had gazed into Jeanne's shining gray eyes, vowing his love before God and before the people.

"I, Antoine de Bourbon, Duke of Vendôme, do solemnly promise to take you, Jeanne of Navarre, as my lawfully wedded wife."

Both Jeanne's parents were present even though neither favored the marriage. Marguerite wept so much before and during the ceremony that it was noted even by the country folk who had come to stare at the bride. When Jeanne tried to comfort her mother by telling her how very happy she was, Marguerite only shook her head.

"I have nothing left to live for. Nothing at all."

Jeanne was silent for a moment. For a fleeting second she felt pity for her mother who refused to share her delight, but then Antoine took her arm.

"Come, ma petite reine. Come and dance with me."

He was dressed so handsomely in a brocaded doublet shining with gold thread, his linen collar edged with lace. His deep brown eyes and gentle touch made up for the coldness and increasing distance between herself and her mother.

Henri d'Albret was in less of a dour mood than his wife, but he was not fond of Antoine either. He had, however, given his consent for the marriage, and for this consent the king of France had promised to pay him 15,000 francs a year. Henri considered Antoine a bit of a dandy, not a real soldier, and one given to spending too much money. For this reason, the morning after the wedding, he stormed into the newlyweds' lodgings and dismissed most of Antoine's servants.

"I've come to trim your feathers," he said to his son-in-law, who took it all good-naturedly enough, "and I've sent your fine gentlemen packing."

Antoine shrugged. He would set the matter right soon enough. He was not afraid of his father-in-law, and for now he was supremely preoccupied with his wife, with Jeanne.

Jeanne for her part could not believe how utterly sweet life was. She had never in her whole life felt so completely loved. She could not look at Antoine without a glow of complete contentment coming over her. *Is he not attractive? Is he not gracious? And is he not married to me?* her heart sang.

Antoine's family was close-knit, and Jeanne envied them. Then she pinched herself because she was now part of his family, and because it seemed that they had taken a liking to her. She was especially drawn to her new sister-in-law, Eléonore Condé, the wife of Antoine's brother. Antoine's relatives often discussed the new faith, and she listened with great interest to their conversations.

The honeymoon months were spent in Béarn. Antoine wanted to explore his wife's native land and enthusiastically threw himself into all the intrigues that Henri of Navarre proposed—intrigues that involved the recapturing of Lower Navarre. Henri, although irritated by the marriage, did find it somewhat satisfying that his son-in-law appeared genuinely interested in Navarre. Antoine, for his part, delighted in playing the future king. He loved riding and walking about the Gascony countryside with Jeanne at his side. With his arm around her waist he imagined that someday, someday this would be his kingdom. Basque was a difficult language. Antoine tried learning it but soon gave up, limiting his words to *bai* for yes and *ez* for no. Jeanne laughed as he tripped over his tongue yet thought no one more clever than her Antoine.

Then their idyllic existence abruptly came to an end. Cousin Henri summoned Antoine to Paris. As the king's word was his command, Antoine prepared to leave. Jeanne, to while away the time, decided to visit her mother who was staying at a health resort.

"My little Jeanne," Antoine said softly on the night before he was to leave.

They were strolling in the terraced gardens of Nérac. Jeanne could not believe how quickly the last six months had passed. She looked up at him.

"Must you really go?"

"I must. Do not be unhappy, sweetheart."

He began to joke upon seeing her downcast face.

"The king commands the dog, and the dog commands the tail."

"That makes me the tail I suppose," she said, but could not help laughing.

Antoine stood a good foot taller than Jeanne, and she leaned against him.

"My little Jeanne," Antoine kissed her ear as he talked, "I never dreamt such happiness as we have would be possible."

She lifted his left hand and rubbed her cheek against it.

"I love you, Antoine."

"And I you, Jeanne," he whispered back, "and will miss you so much."

19
CONVERSATION

"You miss Antoine, don't you?"

Jeanne's mother asked the question with just the hint of a smile in her voice. Jeanne nodded. It was all very well to be with her mother who did seem to enjoy her company right now. But now that she was a wife, a soldier's wife, she did not long for her mother's face anymore but for Antoine's face. Not an hour went by but she had some thought which she wanted to share with him. Her mother coughed. She was very pale. Jeanne felt a pang of guilt that she resented the hours spent with her. Each day was completely taken up with lying in the warm waters of Cauterets. It seemed to somewhat relieve the symptoms of pain which Marguerite had in her joints.

"Do you never miss Father?"

"Yes."

It was a one-word answer, and now that she was married it did not satisfy Jeanne.

"Do you love him?"

Marguerite looked at her without betraying any emotion.

"Your father is married to Navarre," she said, "and after I am gone . . ."

"Maman!"

Jeanne was shocked. It was spring, she was newly married, and all thoughts of death were repugnant to her.

"Surely the waters and the massages you are receiving will help you."

Marguerite had closed her eyes. It was evening, and they were relaxing in her bedchamber. Marguerite, propped up by pillows, lay on top of her bed. The light of the setting sun could be seen through the window, and Jeanne thought of the last time she had watched it with Antoine. Her gaze returned to her mother. She did look ill.

"I know that Yvette's aunt had much pain from rheumatism. But after she took the waters here and was rubbed with the oil of ripe olives mixed with chamomile and rose-dew, even as you are each day, she felt warm and limber. Her sleep much improved, and her general health increased. And so will yours, Maman, in due time."

Her mother did not open her eyes but murmured, "Do you remember your grandmother, Jeanne?"

"A little."

"Well, no matter. She has been gone many years, and you were only a little girl after all when she died. I was there when she died, you know."

"Maman, do not trouble yourself so. Think of other things . . ."

"Before long, Jeanne, we will all be dead, and we will be dead for such a long time beneath the sod."

Jeanne reached out to pat her mother's hands. "You still grieve for Uncle François."

Marguerite's little dog jumped up on the bed and from there onto her belly. Eager for a touch from his mistress, he licked her face. Marguerite opened her eyes and smiled. She patted the dog who, satisfied with the attention, made himself at home on her blue dress.

"I loved your uncle and, indeed, I also loved my mother."

She looked at Jeanne for a while, her eyes searching and, to a certain degree, pleading. Jeanne blushed under the scrutiny and cast her eyes down. She did not speak. Marguerite continued.

"My mother was afraid when she died, did you know that, Jeanne? She was so fearful of death that the physicians were afraid to tell her there was no hope. I do not know what she believed would happen to her. Perhaps she thought purgatory . . ."

Here she stopped, and a large tear rolled down her cheek. It fell on the dog's brown hair, but the creature did not notice. Jeanne stared and swallowed audibly. Marguerite smiled.

"How you have grown, daughter. From such a mischievous child, who cut out the priest's face and put in a fox's face. Perhaps you were wise before your time."

"Why did you never join with the Reformers, Maman? It always seemed you had a foot on the threshold of both religions."

"Let me continue telling you about your grandmother and how she died."

Jeanne sighed. Maman rarely gave straight answers.

"The last rites were administered to her. And after the priests had administered them, Maman called for your Uncle François, but he was not there. He had fled Paris for fear of the plague and was at the royal palace in Blois—he and his children. I told Maman, your grandmaman, that he was not there, and she said, 'It is well that he is not here. It would have been more than either of us could bear. Please leave now, Marguerite. I love you too much to have you stay. I want to fix my thoughts on God alone. Do not trouble me any more now.' And then, a few moments later, before I could gather up enough strength to leave, she was dead."

The clock on the small, ivory inlaid table by the bed ticked and ticked. Marguerite stroked the dog who yawned with pleasure at her touch.

"Why do you tell me this?" Jeanne's voice was hesitant, and she probed carefully.

"Your grandmother," Marguerite answered, "condemned many to the stake. And," she added after a pause, "so did your uncle. They were both . . . both of them afraid to meet their Maker."

Jeanne nervously tapped the fingers of her right hand on the edge of her chair. The shadow of death was so palpable she felt it embrace her. She stood up, wandering over to the window to be closer to the light.

"You will rule well, Jeanne," her mother said. "You will rule well and better than I ever did."

20

SEPARATION

Antoine was recalled to military service while he was in
Paris. Henri I I judged it to be the right time to capture Bou-
logne from the English. Jeanne and Marguerite both returned
to Béarn, Jeanne to Pau and Marguerite to Audos. Both were
despondent, Jeanne because Antoine was off to fight and
Marguerite because she was ill and filled with thoughts of
death.

At the beginning of winter word was sent from Audos to
Pau that Marguerite was failing rapidly. Henri immediately
set out to see her. But he arrived too late. She died before he
could reach her. It shocked Jeanne to see her father weep on
his return. She had never seen him cry and could not recall
that there had been much love between her parents. It made
her long even more desperately for Antoine, who often wrote
her loving letters.

My dear,
Although I wrote at length two days ago I write
again to tell you that I am in as good health as possible.
For it to be perfect I would have to spend a little time

with you. I can hardly wait to see you. I intend another time, when I must take a long trip, to have you with me, for all alone I am discontented.

Marguerite was buried with much splendor near Pau. Several nuns who had cared for her came to pay their last respects and stayed on at the castle a few days. Sister Nicole was one of these, and Jeanne befriended her. She often visited the nun's room, attracted by her quiet demeanor.

"Your mother was a pious woman, I think," Sister Nicole said one evening as they sat together.

"Perhaps," was Jeanne's rather ambiguous answer.

"Are you not certain?" the nun questioned.

Jeanne shook her head.

"She would stroll through the woods at twilight, your mother. And every evening after her stroll she would go into our chapel, kneel down, and pray. Then she would rise and retire to her rooms for the evening accompanied by her ladies. These ladies had nothing but good to say of Madame, your mother, nothing but good."

"What sort of things did they say about her," Jeanne asked, studying the nun.

"Well, they said that she always was interested in what each one was doing. They said she was kind and often gave them gifts to help with family, with marriages . . ."

Sister Nicole stopped when she saw that Jeanne's lips were pursed and that her forehead was wrinkled in thought.

"Is there something that troubles you, child?"

Jeanne shook her head again. How could she tell the kind nun of all the hours that she had, as a child, coveted a kind word or a thoughtful question from her mother? Sister Nicole continued.

"She was dressed very moderately, your mother, not in the manner of the court ladies who vaunt wealth. She always wore a black velvet robe, cut away slightly under the arms. Over that she wore a black jacket with a high sable-lined collar, fastened with brooches at the front. A mob-cap was tucked neatly over her gray hair and often her lap-dog sat on her knees."

Jeanne sat quietly, like a statue, her right hand cupped under her chin, staring off into the distance. In her mind's eye she could see a small child running about a large estate with no one to tend her but servants. When the time came, would she be a better mother than her own had been? She finally broke the silence.

"You touch my mother's outside. I would have you speak to me of her inside. She told me," Jeanne said softly, "the last time I was with her, of a curious event. She said that some years ago . . ."

She paused, searching for the right words before she went on.

". . . some years ago a dear lady-in-waiting was very ill. My mother sat by her bed during her last hours, and when she died, she watched to see if she could discover any sign of her spirit leaving the body. But she told me that she was forced to confess that she had seen nothing at all. Nothing at all."

The nun looked troubled.

"She also wrote a poem," Jeanne continued in a low voice, "in which she said,

> I am conscious neither of body, soul nor life
> without love, and have no desire
> of paradise or fear of hell,

if only unendingly I may be clasped,
united and joined, to my loved one.*

"These words are surely not words of faith. Indeed, I know
not what to think of them. Although . . ." Jeanne hesitated
for a moment before she went on. "Although I think that my
mother was speaking of her brother, whom she loved more
than anyone."

The nun was silent and looked at the floor. Jeanne continued, eager to talk about what bothered her deeply.

"Monsieur Cauvin, the Reformer who is now in Geneva,
was angry with my mother. He wrote to her that he did not
approve of this poem, nor indeed, of some of the other ones
which she wrote these last few years."

"Monsieur Cauvin?"

Sister Nicole suddenly found words and in her impatience
to speak sputtered them all over the room.

"Monsieur Cauvin is far away and a troublemaker, to be
sure. Remember this, child, that your mother caused Latin
prayers to be translated into French. She gave a copy of the
missal to your uncle, King François. Considering that this
translation could have been construed as heresy, it was a dangerous and most courageous thing to do."

Jeanne was silent again. Monsieur Cauvin clearly came to
mind—the thin, earnest man, the man whose whole face had
glowed with joy when he smiled. She was about to respond
that writing or translating prayers was not the same as pray-

*Je me sens corps, âme ne vie,
Sinon amour, et n'ay envie
De paradis, ni d'enfer craincte
Mais que sans fin je sois estraincte
A mon amy, unye et joincte

ing them, when a knock at the door interrupted her train of thought. A servant entered.

"Your husband, Madame, the Duke of Vendôme, has arrived. He is entering the courtyard with his retinue."

At this Jeanne sprang to her feet, all thoughts of faith and death flying out of her head. Antoine was back. Surely now all would be set right.

"She also, Madame, your mother," Sister Nicole continued, unperturbed by the servant, "assisted Monsieur Marot in the translation of the Psalms. As well, she observed Confession, attended Mass, endowed hospitals, founded asylums for orphans, and gave to the poor. Surely these good works will see her to—"

But Jeanne had disappeared, and the theory about being rewarded for good works was left dangling in the air.

21

GOOD NEWS

Early one morning, a few months after her mother's funeral, Jeanne lay awake in bed. She knew she was pregnant. Antoine slept at her side. He looked vulnerable and boyish, and she turned onto her side to study him. They had been married for more than a year now. Softly tracing the lines around his eyes with her fingers, lines that crinkled when he laughed, Jeanne was aware that she knew a great many of his failings now—and still loved him. He was a spendthrift, as her father often told her, and he was also vain, delighting in silken shirts, tight-fitting breeches, and feathered caps. He also gambled and was imprudent in speech, frequently speaking before he thought. But he had a generous heart and agreeable manners, manners that won over most of those with whom he kept company.

The morning air touched her cheeks, inviting her to rise. Turning away from Antoine, and swinging her legs over the edge of their bed, she got up and walked over toward the large, oval mirror on her dresser. She stood quietly, carefully noting her eyes and her mouth. Toinette always said that she could tell if a woman was expecting.

"The eyes are wider," she said, "and the mouth fuller."

Toinette had also said, "A woman who is expecting looks mysterious because carrying a baby is something mysterious which only God fully understands."

Jeanne ran her hand over her cheek. There were circles under her eyes. She didn't really look mysterious, just tired. This was what her mother had hoped for—a grandchild, a grandson, to be more precise. Her mouth quivered. Just once to have heard her say that she herself was the dearest daughter in the world. Antoine's arms suddenly encircled her from behind. He had awoken and gotten out of bed without her hearing anything.

"Why are you up so early, ma petite?"

"I couldn't sleep."

She escaped from his arms and padded over to the window on her bare feet. The vast and well-designed gardens of Pau stretched out before her. Her father and mother had brought the most able gardeners of France to Béarn.

"What is troubling you, Jeanne?"

"Would you still love me even if I never bore you any sons, Antoine?"

"I would love you even if you bore me donkeys!"

He yawned and scratched his back. Always Antoine joked and laughed, and just now Jeanne must hear serious words. Tears formed in her eyes.

"I . . ." she said and could not go on.

Instantly he was at her side.

"Forgive me, ma petite! I spoke in jest. Come, come, don't cry."

He wiped her eyes with the back of his hand. She smiled tremulously.

"I think I am tired. I know you have to go back to make war for Henri in Italy, and I know I will not see you much longer."

"Ah, you know what they say, a fish and a guest go bad on the third day and must be thrown out. I've been here quite a bit longer than . . ."

He stopped because another tear rolled down her cheek. Walking her over to the edge of the bed, he sat her down. Then he knelt in front of her, caressing her hands.

"Jeanne d'Albret, I love you, sons or no sons! You are my beautiful bride and I adore you!"

She smiled, her eyes bright with happiness.

"Yes, I believe you do, sons or not. But in spite of that, here is a little one growing who is thinking about saying hello to his father."

She laid Antoine's hands on her belly, and he, uncomprehending for a second, suddenly laughed out loud.

"Jeanne, my little one!"

He rubbed her belly gently and then laid his cheek against it.

"Bonjour, mon enfant, bonjour."

Then he wept and she loved him the more for it.

Antoine took Jeanne back with him to Paris. From there she sent word to her father that he was to be a grandfather. Henri d'Albret was so delighted with the news that he gave 400 *livres tournois* to the messenger who brought him the letter. When Antoine had to return to active service in mid-summer, he sent Jeanne to Coucy, a nearby feudal fortress. It was a place Antoine could easily visit from his post. In Coucy, one late September afternoon in 1551, Jeanne gave birth to a son. She held the child afterward and gently ran her fingers over the softness of his cheeks, feeling as though no one in the whole world had ever done such a thing as she had just done. What a miracle this new little Henri was, this little Duke de Beaumont, and what a large title for such a little squirmer! She laughed with joy, and Antoine, who was seated on the edge of the bed, laughed with her.

When the little Duke of Beaumont was only a few months old, Antoine encouraged Jeanne to look for a governess. But entranced with her baby's smallness and dependence, she kept him by her side as long as she could. He was baptized with great pomp by an archbishop, and both the king of France and the king of Navarre attended the ceremony. Even as Jeanne had blown milk bubbles during her baptism, so the little duke blew milk bubbles. Gurgling contentedly, he was totally unaware of rank and station.

Antoine, constantly on the move with the French army, traveled to many places, only occasionally able to come to Coucy to see his wife and child. Jeanne was torn between a desire to watch and care for her baby, and a desire to follow her husband from camp to camp. Antoine still wrote letters.

As soon as possible I will come to you with as great anticipation of pleasure as I have ever had in my life. You and our son had better be in good form to welcome me or else I shall make a face and say 'a pu' just as he does. I must see you, either here or there, as I cannot live any longer without you. No husband ever loved a wife as I love you.

In the end it was Jeanne's desire to be with her husband that won out. And she, like her mother before her, appointed Aymée de Lafayette to take care of her baby.

22

DEATH AND LIFE

Jeanne was a wandering bride now. She followed the army, as far as this was possible, as it campaigned in northern France. Meetings with Antoine were hard to arrange, but they contrived to see one another every now and then. When they were not together, there were letters as well as presents.

One morning Jeanne awoke to the sound of barking in her anteroom. Yvette, who had remained her personal attendant, giggled as she opened the heavy curtains to let in the morning light.

"The duke has sent a message . . . and . . ."

She left off talking and handed Jeanne a letter.

Ma petite,

I am sending you a pair of small greyhounds, the prettiest possible, and a linnet, the prettiest and the best talker you've ever seen. I recommend her to you because she loves me so that when I speak she answers, as she does not do to others. That is why I love her.

As for the coming battle, there is nothing to fear—we are in no danger. The enemy is retreating. Furthermore, I assure you that you are more beloved than you have ever been.

Jeanne looked up at Yvette, a slight blush on her cheeks. It made her feel so good for Antoine to say in his letters that he loved her.

"Are the dogs in there?"

She inclined her head toward the outer room. Yvette nodded in delight. She loved the extraordinary, and she doted on the duke. Many of the servant girls did.

Antoine was able to come home for a few months after he sent the gift of the greyhounds. They traveled to Vendôme for a holiday.

"Are you happy, my Jeanne?" Antoine asked.

"Why should I not be? I am twenty-four years old, and I have a handsome husband."

Jeanne answered cheerfully, looking up at him half-shyly as they sat outside on a garden seat. The greyhounds gamboled about on the grass lawn, tumbling over one another in yelping puppyhood.

"And I have," she continued softly, "a healthy son and carry another little one here in my belly. Surely that is happiness."

Antoine took her hand and stroked it.

"You are so good, Jeanne."

"No, I am not," she said. "Often I am afraid."

"Of what are you afraid, ma petite?"

"Oh, I don't know. My mother, she lost her second baby. It was a boy."

She stopped. Antoine had put his finger on her lips. The ruffles on his sleeve tickled her neck.

"Hush," he said, "hush, Jeanne. It is not good to think on death when you are carrying life."

"Yes," she answered, "I know. I know you are right."

The baby kicked. It was a wee kick—a butterfly kick. She smiled and told Antoine so. He grimaced.

"You have such strange thoughts, ma petite. I think we shall be generous with alms. Does not the Lord reward good works?"

"Eléonore says," Jeanne ventured, "that priests want money and that God wants our hearts."

"She is right," Antoine agreed, "but it does no harm to have the priests say extra prayers for us, n'est-ce-pas?"

Jeanne was not convinced but said no more.

Antoine returned to active duty, and the remainder of the summer lay before Jeanne. She felt nauseous and unwell a great deal of the time and regretted that she could not travel far any more. Antoine wanted her to have the baby at Vendôme. It was his birthplace and just north of Plessis-Les-Tours. The days were warm, and Jeanne was restless, unable to relax. One day, just as she was considering a visit to Aymée to see her little son, a messenger arrived, falling on his knees before her.

"On August 20, at the château of La Flêche in Anjou, your child, the young prince Henri, Duc de Beaumont, died. The bishop of Oloron will escort his body here, to Vendôme, for burial."

Jeanne was numb with grief. Antoine was unable to come home to comfort her. After the funeral, she walked about the gardens at Vendôme, her hands on her belly, the wind in her hair, and the sun on her face. She prayed the rosary, she recited the Pater Noster, and she wept until she had no tears left within her. There seemed to be no comfort. Little Henri had been almost two—a happy child, dimpled, and with endearing mannerisms. Why did he have to die? It angered her that Antoine seemed, from his letters, not to grieve as deeply as she did.

> We must not rebel against God's will. I beg you, my dear, not to take this visitation other than as an obedient child. Meanwhile believe that neither this nor anything else would have the power to diminish the love and true affection I bear you.

Jeanne blamed Aymée for her son's death. She reproached herself every day for not going to see little Henri more often and listened to gossips who whispered that the governess had kept all the château windows sealed for fear of cold, thereby depriving her baby of fresh air. Dreaming constantly that she heard little Henri calling out to her that he could not breathe, she would awake with starts knowing that it was too late. Over the course of time, she could not abide Vendôme and traveled south to be with her father.

When Jeanne arrived at the castle of Pau early in December of 1553, she was touched by the fact that her father had willingly prepared her mother's old apartments for her. Tired and sorrowful, she wandered about the rooms, stopping to examine the paintings hanging on the walls, paintings that had been carefully chosen by her mother. Magnificent embroideries as well, crafted by Marguerite and her ladies, decorated various corners. No matter where she sat or looked, Jeanne was reminded of the past. Raphael de Taillevis, Antoine's personal doctor who had traveled with Jeanne, constantly urged her to lie down and rest. Her father, on the other hand, encouraged her to walk the gardens with him, in spite of the cold weather.

"Idleness never made good babies," he said, "and what you need is exercise."

Jeanne, anxious to believe that somewhere deep down her father did love her, walked with him. She studied his face as they strolled and held on to the arm he offered when they climbed some of the rather steep and slippery terraces.

"I've made a will," Henri d'Albret announced curtly as they gazed down on the gardens of Pau. "It's drawn up in your favor," he continued, "and I keep it locked in a secret coffer."

He pulled a golden chain from a bag hanging by his waist. A key hung from it. The chain was long enough to wind about her neck many times. She stared at it as her father dangled it in front of her and then reached out a hand to finger it. It was not that she desired the chain but she wanted to show her father that she knew he was offering her something of great importance to him. December wind tugged at her cloak, and she could not find the words to tell him that she coveted affection rather than a kingdom.

"You can have this chain on two conditions. The first is that you must sing while you give birth to my grandchild. Yes, sing!" he repeated upon seeing her startled face. "I'm sure that if you sing, the child will be healthy."

Jeanne did not answer but studied the landscape. High mountains and steep valleys lay all around—a rugged terrain. Such was life, and she was in a valley now and who would lead her out?

"You must sing a song which invokes the aid of the Virgin Mary."

Jeanne frowned at this. She had spoken often enough now with Eléonore to understand that the Virgin Mary could not help—that only God Himself could help and that through the aid of his Son. Had this Son, she wondered, looked like her own precious son, her little Henri who was now gone?

"Well?" her father demanded.

"I don't know," she began, but he interrupted.

"The second condition is that the child must be a boy, a boy who must be born without a cry from his mother. Meet these conditions, Jeanne, and all that I have will be yours."

He dangled the chain in front of her again, and she closed her eyes for a moment. What did it matter anyway? Antoine would be so pleased if this child would immediately be named the unconditional heir of Navarre. Her father had of late been contemplating remarriage.

"Well?" her father touched her shoulder and then followed her gaze into the distant mountains of Gascony. "It's a beautiful country, is it not, Daughter? *Dudaríkgabe!*—Without doubt! Do you see the vines of Jurançon, the oaks of the Pyrenees, and the snow on the peaks in the distance? It's our country, daughter! Our country!"

He spoke passionately, and Jeanne nodded, for she did deeply love her country. In that she was one with her father.

He patted her belly and lowered his voice confidentially.

"There are accursed Reformers here. I've enacted measures against them. They think to set up churches, but . . ."

He stopped and then added, "Your mother was a fine woman in many ways, but she encouraged these new teachings entirely too much. Everyone now thinks they can come to Béarn and believe what they please."

Jeanne was silent. She knew that her father had never enforced any harsh measures against the new teachings, and that he probably never would. This was not because he had any secret leanings toward the Reformed religion, but because he needed the political support of the many people in Navarre who were Reformed. There were countless merchants, officers, and others who met secretly for worship. Sympathy for the Reformed religion ran high here in Basque country. Her father patted her belly again and repeated his request.

"Well, then you'll sing?"

She nodded.

"Yes, I'll sing."

Ten days after Jeanne was settled in at the castle at Pau, Yvette woke Cotin, a faithful old servant, who slept by the threshold of her apartments.

"Madame Jeanne's time has come."

It was early morning, and the old man tumbled from his pallet and ran as fast as he could first for Dr. Taillevis and then for his master, Henri d'Albret. A rather bleak winter day was dawning, much like the day on which Jeanne had been born some quarter of a century earlier. But Jeanne had no need, as her mother had had so many years before, to walk the floor for hours. Her child was in a hurry. When Jeanne was told that her father was coming, she braced herself. Upon hearing his footsteps in the corridor, she began to sing.

Our Lady at the end of the bridge,
Help me in this present hour.

Pray to the God of heaven that he
Will deliver me speedily
And grant me the gift of a son.

Before she had finished the verse, Jeanne's second child was born. It was another son.

The moment Dr. Taillevis pronounced both mother and child healthy, Henri d'Albret took the baby in his arms.

"A boy! Yes! Yes! It is a boy!" he stuttered in his eagerness to convey his happiness, smiling at Jeanne in a moment of unusual goodwill.

"Well done, girl! Well done!"

He took the gold chain and a coffer from underneath his cape and deposited them on the bed. There was no key.

"My part of the bargain."

He guffawed loudly and dandled the baby. "Well, my grandson. We'll make a true Béarnais lad of you, you'll see."

Producing a piece of garlic from beneath the folds of his robe, he touched the boy's lips. The baby, eyes wide open, after a moment's hesitation, suckled the clove. Henri laughed again in delight.

"A true, true son of Gascony," he said, and then, calling his attendants, "Bring me some of the local Jurançon wine."

When it was brought, he had it poured into a golden goblet. Dipping his finger into the red liquid, he wet the baby's lips. The boy, eyes still open wide, swallowed the wine easily and seemed content.

"A true Béarnais," the king repeated, "a true Béarnais."

Later that day, Henri d'Albret held the infant prince in his arms by a window. Many of the local nobles, as well as lesser folk, were assembled on the lawns of Pau. Years before, when Jeanne was born, the Spaniards had mocked her birth, saying, "The bull has sired a lamb!"

Opening the window in a gesture of triumph, Henri shouted down for all people to hear.

"Look! The lamb has given birth to a lion!"

23

Matters of the Heart

Henri d'Albret took his grandson and settled him in the countryside of Béarn at the château of Coarraze near the small village of Nay. Distant cousins owned this château, and they were happy to have the care of a baby boy. Small Henri, for he was given the name of his dead brother, was a fussy child, and seven wet-nurses were tried before one was found whose milk agreed with his royal stomach. Jeanne spent much time at Coarraze. She sat by the cradle, which had been beautifully crafted out of tortoise shell, and rocked her little son for hours on end, every now and then reaching in to touch his soft skin. Firelight colored his round cheeks rosy. He looked so snug and cozy, small fists tightly clasping the edge of the blanket, that it was all Jeanne could do to keep from snatching him up and hugging him. He would be dark-haired like his father. Softly singing a Navarre lullaby, she leaned back in her chair.

Binbili, bonbolo, go to sleep,
If we were in France

The ass would drum
The ox would dance
And the goat would play the tambourine.

Someone behind her discreetly coughed. Startled, for she had thought she was by herself, she turned her head. It was the wet-nurse.

"Is it time for his feeding?"

The woman nodded, and Jeanne bent over to lift Henri out of the cradle. The left side of his cheek was crinkled and red with sleep. He whimpered, his mouth puckering threateningly. Jeanne held him close for a moment as the woman sat down opposite her and opened her shift. She then handed him over. They both smiled at the baby's enthusiasm for his meal. He drank noisily, swallowing great gulps of milk. Jeanne recalled Toinette who had taken such loving care of her as a child. Watching the nurse's face carefully, she noted that the woman was genuinely fond of Henri. It was a relief to her, especially since Antoine was impatient to have her back at his side.

Jeanne returned to Coarraze as often as she could, and each visit she marveled at the miracle of growth that had taken place in her absence. It seemed that in no time at all Henri changed from a helpless baby into a fast crawler, and from a fast crawler into a sturdy toddler who could run about barefoot on the grass and climb onto rocks. His grandfather saw to it no one pampered him or treated him as a prince. He received no toys, and after he was weaned, his food consisted of brown bread, beef, cheese, and garlic.

By the time little Henri began to crawl, Jeanne knew she was expecting again. Toward the end of this pregnancy she retired to an estate in Normandy where Antoine was stationed. Little Henri stayed behind in Coarraze under the strict supervision of his grandfather. Jeanne was confident the little boy was being cared for with love and wisdom. Heavy with this third baby, she waited for the birth anxiously. Motherhood always turned her thoughts to her own mother, always made her ask questions to which she had never been able to get an answer. Why had Marguerite hesitated between the two religions? Why had she supported the Reformers but never joined them? Why had she criticized the Roman Catholic Church but never left it? Could a person believe two opposing faiths at the same time? She felt the new baby move in her belly. It grew there, and sooner or later she would have to bring it forth. Was it not the same with a belief? she pondered. Did it not grow like a child within you, sooner or later to be born and to be nurtured?

A third son, the little Comte de Marle, was born in Normandy. Antoine and Jeanne traveled down to Pau with the healthy baby when he was only a few weeks old so his grandfather could see him. Henri d'Albret was as delighted with this baby as he was with Henri. Two grandsons! What wealth! Jovially he invited his daughter and her husband to go hunting with him. Antoine was pleased. He loved the hunt and owned many horses and falcons. Riding side by side with his father-in-law, he cheerfully waved to the local people. Noting Henri d'Albret's aging and worn face, he thought to himself that it would not be too much longer before he would reign in these parts. It was a good hunt, and even though it was not

Jeanne's favorite pastime, she was happy to see her father and husband amicably riding side by side.

When they returned to the castle at Pau, the new little Comte de Marle was peevish and would not stop crying. Swaddled tightly, he wailed loudly enough to bring both Jeanne and Antoine to the nursery. Antoine was suspicious.

"What ails the baby?"

"He is merely fussy, my lord, and should fall asleep soon."

But in the morning the child was dead in the tortoise shell cradle, and when Jeanne took off his swaddling clothes, she discovered a bruised little body with many broken bones.

In a letter to Eléonore, Jeanne poured out her grief.

The little one was such a fine baby. Everyone wanted to hold him. My father was much pleased at his size and his alertness. While we were out hunting with my father, one of the gentlemen-in-waiting and the nurse who was taking care of him amused themselves by tossing him back and forth across the sill of an open window. Sometimes they would pretend not to catch him. This was the cause of the tragedy that resulted, because the nurse, expecting that the gentleman would catch him, although he pretended that he would not, let the baby go and my little one fell and hit a stone step below, on which he broke some ribs. This was all kept secret from us. I believe the baby might have been saved if I had known. My father blames me. He looks at me and looks at me. But it is the eye of my inward parts, the eye of my conscience which haunts me.

After the funeral, Antoine returned to active military duty. Jeanne was still desperate with grief. She prayed. But her Pater Nosters and Hail Marys were no help. It mattered not whether she recited them all day, they gave no relief to the aching void and guilt she carried.

Eléonore wrote her a long letter.

My dear sister:

... Approach him who is the Greatest Physician of all. Yes, you yourself should approach Him. A priest or a saint cannot do this for you. Kneel in front of your bed, my dear sister, and tell Him all. He cares and He hears and He comforts ...

After Yvette left the room that evening, Jeanne did as Eléonore suggested. She knelt down by her bed and prayed and wept all in one. And the truth was that praying in this manner gave her a sense of God's presence and comfort—a presence sweeter than Antoine's body holding her close and a comfort dearer than his kisses.

One evening after Jeanne had dismissed her women, as Yvette helped her into her nightgown, the servant was unusually quiet. Jeanne, who was used to her chattering, asked what was the matter.

"I have just had word from Monsieur Marcel, my cousin, that my uncle . . ." Yvette began, and then shivered, "that my uncle died. He was a tailor in Paris."

Jeanne studied Yvette's face in the mirror. She had not heard the girl speak of her uncle before, but she was pale and truly upset.

"I am sorry," she said.

"He was a good man," Yvette went on, as she brushed Jeanne's hair with long, careful strokes. "And he was accused of eating meat on a Friday."

Jeanne was quiet, surprised that the girl had relatives of the new faith.

"My uncle was summoned with three others to stand before King Henri. My cousin said he was not afraid. He was not a tall man, my uncle. He was shorter than I am."

Yvette stopped her work and put her left hand to her right shoulder.

"That is how tall he was, my Uncle Armand."

Jeanne nodded.

"When he was questioned by the bishops who were with the king, he answered them very well. They could not make sport of him no matter how much they tried. Then the king's mistress, Diane Poitiers, began to mock his faith, and my uncle . . ."

She stopped and looked down before she finished in a soft voice, a voice very unlike the Yvette Jeanne knew, ". . . my uncle said to Diane Poitiers, 'Be satisfied, Madam, with having infected France, without mingling your filth in a matter so holy and sacred as the religion of our Lord Jesus Christ.' "

Jeanne sucked in her breath at the courage of the little tailor and bade Yvette to continue.

"The king himself watched my uncle's burning at the stake. He had a special window made so he could watch his agony from close by and rejoice in his pain. But this is what happened. My uncle looked up at the window and saw the king. Although flames engulfed him, he would not turn his gaze away. The king, it is reported, tried to walk away from the window, but my uncle's eyes held him. After the execution, the king could not sleep. My uncle's eyes haunted him. Even so, I cannot sleep for I think of my uncle constantly. Oh, Madame, truly his faith was holy and good and—"

Yvette broke down and sobbed. Jeanne stood up and patted her on the shoulder.

"It is all over, Yvette. And it does my cousin, the king, no harm at all to have his conscience pricked. Perhaps it will frighten him away from these wicked executions. Perhaps it will spur him on to read the Bible."

Yvette's cries grew softer, and Jeanne went on, speaking to herself now.

"Perhaps that is where conscience now also directs me."

24

TRAVELS

Only a few months after the death of her third child, Jeanne's father also died while preparing for yet another campaign against Spain to recapture Spanish Navarre. Jeanne and Antoine inherited his earthly kingdom.

With something akin to horror, Jeanne soon noted that Antoine did not love Navarre as she did. As a butcher bargains with a piece of meat, so he bargained over it without her knowledge. In exchange for a portion of Navarre, Antoine asked Cousin Henri for some property in the middle of France. Even though the deal did not materialize, Jeanne was outraged, and they quarreled. It was their first quarrel. Antoine quickly forgot and laughed as he always did, but Jeanne found it difficult to forget his dishonorable act.

She was expecting yet another child and wondered if this little one would live. God seemed pleased to give her children, but he seemed just as pleased to take them back. Often, with her ladies at her side, and a small company of soldiers as guard, she traveled to visit little Henri at Coarraze in the valley of Lourdes. She had to reassure herself again and again of his health. The child spoke the Basque language and much amused the ladies who had come with her. One day they sat together in a glen.

"*Bat, bij, yron, lae, boss*—one, two, three, four, five," the child proudly counted flowers on his chubby fingers and gallantly he offered a bunch to Jeanne, bowing his square little body as he did so.

"*Noa*, I go," he said."

"Where do you go, my son?"

He pointed to a butterfly. His childish, merry voice pronounced the word correctly,

"*Pimpirina.*"

Jeanne laughed, as did her ladies. They watched him climb the rocks with uncovered head and bare feet, and Jeanne's heart swelled with pride at his sturdy form. She thought of how she would also train his mind to be as healthy as his body. There must be no confusion for him. She would provide good tutors—tutors of the Reformed religion so that he would learn the truth. She had spoken with Antoine about these things, and he did not object. Indeed, there were a number of pastors from Geneva at their court now who taught freely. Each Sunday Jeanne, Yvette, and others in her retinue heard them preach. Creation, the Fall and the redeeming love of Jesus Christ became a constant sweet message to them, and many began to believe and understand the Gospel.

As Henri scrambled on the rocks, an old Basque shepherd appeared from behind a slope. His broad but rounded shoulders and angular features typified many of Navarre's subjects. Henri ran up to him, obviously well acquainted with the man.

"Play, Barbot, please play!"

The man patted the child's head and then sat down by a bush as Henri stood nearby. He had an elongated, wooden box strapped to his back. With great care he took it off and lifted it onto his right knee. Jeanne saw that it was a *ttun-ttun*, or *tambourin de Gascogne*. The man also put a *tchirula*, a three-holed pipe, to his mouth. He began to play a cheerful tune on the pipe, at the same time keeping up a rhythmic thrumming with a little stick on the *ttun-ttun*. Henri was delighted and gleefully danced in the grass for the ladies. They laughed and clapped their hands. It was a cheerful picture and one which Jeanne carried in her heart as she returned to Pau.

Jeanne's next baby, a little girl, was named Magdelaine and only lived for two weeks. It was another sorrow Jeanne bore and hid in her heart. Antoine was sad as well, but able to forget quickly, too quickly. Anxious now to have little Henri near her, she had him taken from Coarraze to the castle at Pau and appointed a governess. But the governess was not Aymée. Aymée had been dismissed. Jeanne's confidence in her had been destroyed by the death of her first little son.

"We shall go to court." Antoine announced one day.

"Why?" Jeanne absently stared at her husband, who walked through their apartments with an air of excitement.

"Well, it is time for our young Henri to be presented to your cousin, the king of France. It is only proper. Also, it is a good opportunity to properly show ourselves as king and queen of Navarre as we travel through all our territories."

Antoine walked over to Jeanne, clasping her hands in his.

"It is a good way to inspire loyalty in our subjects, Jeanne. People will see us together with our child, and they will love us. Don't you think so?"

Jeanne nodded. It was a wise idea and Antoine's charm, when he wanted to show it, always made a favorable impression on the people he met.

They left for the French court in the middle of November, traveling in short stages from city to city. The weather was unusually mild, and Antoine, when they approached large cities, dressed up in a rich tunic. Enjoying himself immensely, he rode a magnificent white horse caparisoned even as he was. Jeanne, at his side, was also dressed splendidly in a dress of gold cloth trimmed with ermine and adorned with precious stones. Little Henri stole everyone's hearts with his mischievous grins and enthusiastic waves. Everywhere they went they were cheered and presented with keys of the cities. Eventually, with much pomp, they reached Paris and cousin Henri.

The audience with the king began awkwardly.

"Your Majesty," Antoine said and bowed before the French king who stared at him somewhat distrustfully. He did not like it when others appeared more popular or royal than he did, and he had heard that even Paris had warmed to the Navarre royal couple. Sulking somewhat, therefore, he chose not to speak or acknowledge Antoine's greeting. Jeanne likewise bowed, kissing her cousin's hand. But Henri II, even as his father, François I, before him, had no fondness for the kingdom of Navarre. He feared that Antoine and Jeanne would plot and connive with Spain against France. There was a silence, and it became an uncomfortable silence. Henri II continued to ignore them. Antoine coughed into his hand, for once at a loss for words. Suddenly behind them, little Henri, who had been left in another room with his governess, burst in through the door. He ran as fast as his three-year-old feet could carry him and made straight for the king of France, grabbing his knees and holding on tightly.

"Who are you?" Henri II asked, bewildered by the small bundle of boy hanging onto him.

"Henri of Navarre," the lad promptly replied, looking up without fear, "and who are you?"

"Henri of France."

Small Henri smiled openly, let go of the royal knees and stood up, unabashedly staring. Henri II reached out his arms and took the child on his lap. He was fond of children.

"Would you like to be my son?" he said, half in jest and half in earnest.

"*A quet es lo seigne pay*, that gentleman is my father," the boy replied in the Béarnais patois, pointing to Antoine.

"Well then, I think you must be my son-in-law. Would you like that?"

Henri dimpled and nodded in agreement.

"*O bai*, oh, yes!"

King Henri laughed, amused by the child, and now began chatting amiably with his parents. But Jeanne remained uncomfortable throughout the interview, not able to forget the fact that here was a man who burned heretics as easily as he changed his white linen shirts. And she shuddered inwardly to see little Henri on his lap.

"It seems," said Henri II, as if he could read Jeanne's thoughts, stroking the child's hair all the time, "that all of France is infected with the heresy of the Reformers. In every town, province, and trade this wickedness has taken root. How is it with you, Antoine?"

Antoine inclined his head and frowned, as if disturbed by Henri's words.

"I am of the same faith and opinion as Your Majesty," he answered smoothly.

"I hear that your brother, Prince of Condé, and that your uncles, Gaspard de Coligny and d'Andelot, are of the new opinions. How come you to be in such a . . ."

He stopped as little Henri pulled at his beard. Jeanne smiled within herself. That is what she would like to do, pull Cousin Henri's beard.

". . . such a," Henri continued, "pagan family."

Jeanne turned red. This was an insult to Antoine's honor, and she fully expected him to take Henri to task. But she was disappointed.

"I am sure, Your Majesty," Antoine said slowly, "that you will find Navarre a most obedient and loyal servant to yourself."

It was more than Jeanne could bear. She walked over to the king and held out her arms for the child. Little Henri willingly complied, for he loved his mother. Then she walked out of the room with her head held high.

25

GROWTH

In spite of what Antoine had so glibly said to King Henri II, Navarre continued to be a haven for the new religion. Both Antoine and Jeanne regularly attended Reformed services, and they also appointed a Monsieur Boisnormand as their minister. A learned man, skilled in Hebrew, he often discussed faith with Antoine. But the king of Navarre never fully committed himself to the new teachings. The truth was that he was afraid. The pope had sent him a message threatening him with excommunication.

Jeanne, on the other hand, had no such fears and marveled at the feeling of happiness that washed over her whenever she heard God's Word explained. She wrote to a friend.

Up to now I have followed in the footsteps of the deceased queen, my most honored mother, whom God forgive, in the matter of hesitation between the two religions. She was warned by her brother the king not to get new doctrines in her head. I well remember how long ago, the late king, my most honored father, surprised my mother when she was praying in her rooms with the ministers Roussel and Farel, and how with great annoyance he slapped her right cheek and forbade her sharply to meddle in matters of doctrine. He shook a stick at me which cost me many bitter tears. Now that I am freed by the death of my father, a reform seems so right and so necessary that, for my part, I consider that it would be disloyalty and cowardice to God, to my conscience, and to my people to remain any longer in a state of suspense and indecision.

There was for Jeanne not only the joy of realizing more and more that she was a child of God, but there was also the joy in knowing that she was once again expecting new life in her womb.

One day as Antoine and Jeanne rode together on the country paths of Béarn, she said, "I am going to have another baby, Antoine."

It seemed as if Antoine had not heard her. A small retinue of courtiers trailed behind. The not-too-distant Pyrenees rose enormous at their side. Slowly picking her way through a tangle of sweet-smelling bracken that had overgrown onto the road, Jeanne repeated the words, this time making her sentence plural.

"We are going to have another baby."

Antoine moved his gaze from the slopes above them and nudged his horse closer.

"I heard you, ma petite, and I am glad."

She smiled, relieved at his words. A chamois (a small antelope) jumped across the path a few meters ahead of them. The animal's agility was both remarkable and fleeting, for a moment later it had disappeared without trace into the undergrowth.

"We are much like the *isards*, the chamois, are we not," said Jeanne dreamily, "one brief jump, a few seconds on the path, and then we are gone."

Antoine laughed loudly. "You silly goose! I shall never understand you completely. Chamois, indeed! We are alive and shall live for a long time if we take care. Just look at the mountains and gaze at the valleys rich with wine and oil and forest. Doesn't looking at them make you feel strong?"

Jeanne felt a trifle foolish and didn't know what to say in reply. Antoine urged his horse on ahead of her. She had hoped to speak to him about her fears, to tell him that she was afraid that this child, like the others, might die. She gazed up at the Pyrenees as he had suggested. Solid, one unbroken line, they brushed the sky with their tips. Softly murmuring, Jeanne prodded her horse to follow Antoine. She recalled the words Monsieur Boisnormand had advised her to memorize and say whenever she was troubled.

My heart is sore pained within me: and the terrors of death are fallen upon me. Fearfulness and trembling are come upon me, and horror hath overwhelmed me. And I said, Oh, that I had wings like a dove! for then would I fly away, and be at rest. Lo, then would I wander far off, and remain in the wilderness. I would hasten my escape from the windy storm and tempest.

Her heart lifted somewhat, and she resolved that she would speak to Antoine. He was her husband, after all, and the father of her children.

Later that week Jeanne did voice her worries. But although Antoine kissed her and held her close for a moment, he would not take her seriously.

"You are my little saint," he said, with a certain amount of exasperation. "But you must laugh more. You must forget the Bible sometimes. I almost think it has become your third arm, the way you carry it about. Come, come. Have some fun with me, ma petite, and then I am sure you will feel better."

On a blustery day in February, Jeanne gave birth to a beautiful little girl. She was named Catherine, and she had a healthy appetite as well as a cry that traveled the length of the castle's corridor. She was, indeed, a lusty little princess. Fair, downy hair crowned a sweet, pixie face.

"She is perfect," Antoine said a week after her birth, slightly in awe of the smallness of his daughter.

"*And* she is ours," Jeanne answered with a smile, but then feeling guilty added, "given to us by God himself."

"Well, gift or not," Antoine answered, "she is perfect."

He dandled her and called her "little woman" until she burped milk onto his doublet. At this point Jeanne doubled over with laughter on their big four-poster bed. Antoine laughed too, and for a few weeks it seemed as if there were no problems. And then Cousin Henri called a *Mercuriale*, in Paris.

Because he was a Prince of the Blood and a *Mercuriale* was a meeting of the leaders of France, Antoine also received an invitation to attend. He read it with some misgiving. Was it a trap? Had the pope denounced him? Did Henri suspect that he was aiding Reformers?

"Do not go!" Jeanne cautioned him. "Stay here."

But Antoine, afraid of risking King Henri's anger, traveled to Paris in haste.

Many important nobles attended the *Mercuriale*. Antoine took care where he sat in the great hall where the meeting took place, seeking safety in the respectability of old Senator du Bourg. The senator smiled at him as he sat down, asking him about Jeanne's health and that of the new baby. But Antoine was unable to answer the man's courteous inquiries as Henri II, at that moment, entered with much pomp. Taking his place on the prepared throne, he was all-powerful majesty, with the royal archers in their colorful uniforms surrounding him. There was silence until Henri, carefully arranging his crimson robes about him, began to speak.

"I have called you here," his voice rang loudly and authoritatively, "to say that we must vote to reaffirm total allegiance to the pope, who is God's representative on earth."

If it was quiet before, it was now deathly quiet. Some of the senators looked at one another in consternation. Antoine licked his dry lips and silently wondered for the hundredth time if Henri knew about the Reformed services that were being held in Pau every Sunday, or if he was aware that thousands of people in Navarre loved the preaching of the Reformed pastors who had been sent there by Geneva.

"My daughter, Elizabeth," Henri continued, his voice rising as he spoke, "will soon be married to Philip of Spain. You all know that this great monarch hates heretics and burns all those who will not invoke the Virgin Mary. We are at one with Spain in this. I hereby admonish every one here to rout out the heretics; to hunt them down; and to kill every last one of them."

Antoine had no particular quarrel with those of the new religion, but neither did he have any inclination to defend them. Morosely he looked at the ground and wished that he had not come.

"The matter of heresy," one senator ventured, looking up at the king as he spoke, "is presently being discussed at the Council of Trent. We do well to wait for the outcome of the council's decrees on this issue."

The senator's words encouraged others to speak up, and none was more eloquent than Antoine's neighbor, old Annas de Bourg. He stood as he spoke, while Antoine kept his eyes glued to the marble floor, wishing he had sat somewhere else.

"Your Majesty," du Bourg said, inclining his head respectfully to Henri, "there are many wicked crimes today, crimes such as adultery, lying, and profanity, which are never punished. And yet these Reformers, these 'heretics' you speak of, whose only crime is that they pray for you, will be punished by torture and stake. Should not torture and stake be reserved for those who rebel against Your Majesty?"

He stopped, and Henri II eyed him coldly. Annas du Bourg calmly went on.

"Your Majesty," he said, "it is a grave matter to condemn to the flames men who die calling on the name of the Lord Jesus."

Antoine cringed, knowing that the senator had now probably signed his death warrant. He avoided du Bourg's eye as he looked around the room, waiting for others to back him up.

"The votes, gentlemen," Henri abruptly ended the session, not giving anyone else a chance to speak, "it is time for the votes."

The votes of everyone present were marked in a book, a book which the king carefully checked. The archers in their uniforms stood around him, bows slung across their shoulders. Fleetingly Antoine remembered the chamois and Jeanne's words—"one brief jump, a few seconds on the path, and then we are gone."

Henri closed the book with a bang. Then he stood up with anger written all over his face.

"Traitor!"

He pointed a long, white finger at du Bourg.

"Arrest him!"

The Constable of France immediately marched over to du Bourg who did not appear afraid.

"Give my regards to Madame Jeanne, your wife," he said to Antoine.

Antoine nodded briefly, numb with dismay. Later that day he heard that the old senator had been taken to the Bastille by the Captain of the Guard, and shut up in an iron cage to await sentencing.

As Antoine traveled home, he was truly upset that matters of religion could so affect life. Faith, he contemplated, was relative. In Paris, he had been a Roman Catholic, and in Navarre he would probably be in agreement with the Reformers again. Life was not certain, and surely God was present in both religions. Digging his spurs into the sides of his horse, he thought that Jeanne was becoming too serious these days and not at all the fun-loving bride she had been a few years ago.

His thoughts drifted to the pretty ladies-in-waiting that Catherine de Médicis, Henri II's wife, had introduced him to just this last week. Catherine was not such a bad queen. Jeanne did not like her, but Catherine had certainly understood that he, Antoine, needed a little extra affection every now and then. But the smooth, gray pebbles at the wayside kicked up by the horse's hoofs reminded him of Jeanne's eyes. And those eyes reproached him more with each mile. To quiet his conscience, he began to sing a boisterous tavern song. But the tune did not take away the truth that he would soon have to defend the fact that he had not spoken up for du Bourg.

A month after Antoine's visit to Paris news arrived at Pau that King Henri had died while celebrating the marriage of his daughter Elizabeth to Philip of Spain. Jousting with the same captain of the guard who had taken du Bourg to prison, he had been involved in an accident. The captain's lance had struck his visor with such force that it had flown open, splinters of the lance piercing his eye and penetrating to his brain. The king reeled to and fro to keep himself on horseback, but the injury was too severe. He soon fell to the ground and was carried off the field. He died ten days later in much pain.

"Was his death divine justice?"
Jeanne asked Antoine the question while they were out walking in the gardens of Pau. The flowered terraces were in full bloom. The newly mown lawn smelled fresh.
"They say," she went on, "that the palace, which was decorated for his daughter's wedding, is now draped in black and that Henri's corpse is covered with a magnificent cloth."
Antoine shrugged. In the distance they could see their son frolicking about on a small pony, a groomsman running along at his side. Antoine laughed and pointed. But Jeanne was not to be diverted.

"It seems rather humorous, but also frightening, don't you think, Antoine, that the conversion of Paul was depicted on the cloth that covered Cousin Henri's body and large letters were embroidered on it. The letters read 'Saul, Saul, why do you persecute me?'"

Antoine did not answer. He concentrated instead on the clearness of the day, the beauty of the landscape, and the wealth of his position. But in the evening, when night fell, he nervously whistled in the dark as he walked about the castle's corridors. Death had obviously caught cousin Henri, a chamois in mid-air, unaware.

26

REFUGE

Antoine traveled back to Paris for the coronation of Henri's son, François II. François was a boy of sixteen summers. Not strong physically or mentally, he was married to the beautiful Scottish princess, Mary Stewart. Mary's uncles, the French Guise brothers, exercised much influence on the new young king of France.

Jeanne did not go to the coronation with Antoine. She preferred to stay home to supervise small Henri's education and to see to it that baby Catherine was properly taken care of. The children were the light of her life.

"Why did Papa have to leave again, Maman?"

Henri asked the question many times. He loved his carefree father—a father who would throw him high up into the air and play mock sword-battles with him.

"He is gone to Paris, and you know very well why he went."

Jeanne sighed as she answered, knowing that the child would ask again tomorrow.

"Why couldn't the new king be crowned without him?" Henri persisted.

"Because your papa is a Prince of the Blood, and that makes him a very important man in France."

Henri smiled. He liked hearing that his father was important. Indeed, he thought his father the most important man in the whole world.

"Will he bring me a present when he comes back? Perhaps a sword?"

Jeanne frowned and shook her head.

"You do well to study your books, young man! And I don't want to hear any more talk about swords."

Antoine came back from the coronation rather subdued. He had been snubbed in Paris. The queen mother, Catherine de Médicis, had ignored him; the young king himself had refused to speak with him; and his place in the coronation procession had been at the tail end. He was worried about his future and moped about the castle.

"What is troubling you so much?" Jeanne whispered the words from her side of the bed.

She wanted Antoine to confide in her. She wanted him to say that nothing mattered except the fact that they were together and that they ruled a wonderful kingdom.

"I don't know," Antoine replied as he pounded his pillow into shape, "There are so many changes taking place that a man doesn't know whom to depend on anymore."

"There are reports trickling in from the north," Jeanne said, as she raised herself up on one elbow, looking her husband full in the face. "And they say that those who rejoiced at my cousin Henri's death, are now thinking that perhaps things were easy under him."

"It's those cursed Guise brothers," Antoine scowled. "They tell François what to do, and they're out to get everyone who stands in their way."

He stopped and took Jeanne's hand, a nervous tic appearing in his cheek.

"They're out to get us as well, Jeanne."

"We are safe here," she reassured him. "My father spent much time and money on the fortress Navarreux."

He sighed and let go of her hand, answering with something like pity. "That may be, but we cannot hide in a fortress for the rest of our lives."

"We do not hide," Jeanne replied, a hot surge of anger coursing over her. "Navarre never hides. We are a proud country."

Antoine patted her hand. "I know. I know. But I will be summoned to court again before long, mark my words, and I cannot take the fortress with me."

"Well, then do not obey if you are summoned. You are a monarch in your own right here in Navarre."

Antoine sighed, turned away and pulled the covers over him. Jeanne lived in a world that was too small for him. She was in too confined a space. He fell asleep thinking that Paris, for all its dangers, had many attractions he wanted to enjoy. Jeanne did not fall asleep but studied his hunched up form for a long time by the flickering candlelight. He was her husband and she still loved him in spite of all his failings. But she was not at all sure that he still loved her and Navarre.

The next few months many Protestant refugees traveled to Navarre from France, people whose houses had been demolished and who had lost everything they owned. Jeanne spoke to one such man, an older fellow with a long beard, as he rested in her courtyard.

"Well, father," she said kindly, "what brings you here?"

"My wife and children were murdered," he answered in a voice heavy with emotion.

"I am sorry," she said. "Why and by whom?"

But she knew the answer before he gave it.

"By the king's soldiers, or should I say by Guise soldiers? My wife and two daughters passed an image of the Virgin Mary. It had been set up on a street corner. Guards were posted nearby to watch for heretics. They arrested anyone who did not genuflect or stop to kneel. My wife and daughters knew better than to bow to an idol."

He stopped and small Henri, who had been standing at his mother's side, balled his fists and cried out, "Ah, Maman, this is why I want to learn how to fight properly. So that I can avenge—"

"Hush," Jeanne said, covering Henri's mouth with her hand, "you don't know what you are saying."

"No, he does not," the old man said, "for it is God's to avenge."

He stopped and bit his lip, not wishing to weep before a woman and a boy. Jeanne put her arm around his shoulder.

"You are safe here, old father. My country . . ."

She faltered, overcome by a jumble of thoughts. What if Antoine and Henri and Catherine died? How would she feel? And what exactly did her country stand for? What did she herself stand for? Monsieur Cauvin had written that enemies of God, enemies such as the Guise brothers and the young king, François, could only be fought with prayer and patience.

The old man gently disengaged himself from her embrace and smiled at her kindly.

"I will stay here in Basque country," he said. "It was the country of my father and my uncles. My relatives will put me up. I've come back to die here. Thank you for giving so many shelter."

Small Henri, still at Jeanne's side, doffed his cap and bowed to the grandfather.

"*Gangon díssíla*," he said, "God give you good evening."

The soft resonance of the Basque tongue sounded sweet to Jeanne's ears. Henri was increasingly proficient in the language of his country. He put his sturdy hand in that of his mother, and together they watched the old man trudge off through the courtyard toward the drawbridge.

Yvette, who had been zealous for the Reformed cause since her uncle's death and who was still privy to all the news from Paris, heard how brave du Bourg had died.

"Du Bourg," she said to Jeanne and the other ladies in the room, as they were sewing one snowy afternoon, "was shut up in an iron cage and fed nothing but bread and water. Yet it is known that he constantly sang psalms. His trial was a mockery, and he was condemned before any evidence was given."

"Yvette," Jeanne spoke softly, "Yvette, do not upset yourself so."

The girl was red with agitation, and she stood in the middle of the chamber with clenched hands. Her embroidery had fallen on the floor. For once she did not listen to Jeanne and went on.

"He was burned in Paris two days before Christmas. The wicked Guise brothers were there and cheered. But they could not stop his steadfastness and courage. And he turned many to the true religion."

Weeping she bent over to pick up her sewing, but her hands shook so that another lady kindly stood up to help her.

Isabelle, another of Jeanne's ladies-in-waiting, took up the story where Yvette had left off. She pulled a piece of paper from her pocket.

"Someone sent me Senator du Bourg's words, words he spoke before he died."

She began to read slowly but very clearly:

None shall be able to separate us from Christ, whatever snares are laid for us, whatever ills our bodies may endure. We know that we have long been like lambs led to the slaughter. Let them, therefore, slay us. Let them break us to pieces; for all that, the Lord's dead will not cease to live, and we shall rise in a common resurrection. I am a Christian! Yes, I am a Christian! I will cry yet louder when I die, for the glory of my Lord Jesus Christ! And since it is so, why do I tarry? Lay hands upon me, executioner, and lead me to the gallows!

She swallowed back tears before she was able to continue. Most of the ladies were weeping.

Put an end, put an end to your burnings, and return to the Lord with amendment of life, that your sins may be wiped away. Let the wicked forsake his way and the unrighteous man his thoughts and let him return unto the Lord and he will have mercy upon him. Live, then, and meditate upon this, O senators; and I go to die!

Yvette now sobbed audibly and blew her nose.

"He was taken," Isabelle continued as she folded the paper and put it back into her pocket, "to the Place de Grève. Many people were there to witness his death. 'My friends', he cried, 'I am here not as a thief or robber, but for the gospel.' And he spoke to them of the love Christ has for sinners who repent and believe in him. Then, before he died, he exclaimed again and again, 'My God, forsake me not, that I may not forsake thee!' "

Yvette spoke again, her voice thick with tears.

"I have heard that every day soldiers carry people of all ages and ranks off to prison. The streets are so crowded with carts loaded with the furniture of these poor people that it is hardly possible to walk in Paris. Children wander about whose parents have been taken. They cry for bread, yet no one gives them even a morsel because the new religion is so hated."

"Hush," Jeanne said, "It does us no good to speak of these things."

They all looked at her and she blushed. She felt, as all her ladies did, compassion for the Huguenots.

"If crops are destroyed, or hail falls, or disease strikes," she said softly, looking around with affection, "it is said to be the fault of the Protestants. The Guise brothers whisper these things and people repeat them. But the Guise brothers lie. They incite the young King François to persecute good people and to take their land in God's name. If only, oh, if only someone would guide the young king in the right manner."

Jeanne was not the only one who realized that François was a very young king, indeed, and that he needed to be away from the influence of his scheming uncles. In the spring of

1560 a plot to kidnap the king away from his wicked advisors failed. Antoine's brother, the Prince de Condé, Eléonore's husband, was rumored to be the secret leader of the Conspiracy of Amboise, as the plot became known. But he denied it and then immediately traveled to the safety of Navarre to be with Antoine and Jeanne.

27

A KING'S COMMAND

"Why does King François believe that you tried to kidnap him?" Little Henri of Navarre stood in front of his Uncle Condé who had just arrived.

"Because the king believes anything those blackguard Guise brothers whisper in his ear!"

"But you told the truth?" Henri said, steadily looking at his father's brother.

He couldn't believe that such a man as his Uncle Condé, dressed in a rich tunic with sleeves of velvet, could be in trouble.

"Indeed, I did, my fine Nephew. I told the truth. I told the king that he had my loyalty and that I have always served the crown, as he knows. And I said that whoever accused me of treason had lied. And when I said this, my boy, I looked straight at the Duke of Guise who was so affronted he almost spit in my face."

Henri laughed but quickly sobered.

"And then what happened, Uncle?"

"Well, then I mounted the swiftest horse I could find and rode down to Béarn as I did not think it safe to remain at Chenonceaux."

Henri nodded with all the understanding his seven years could muster. He had heard, as everyone in Béarn had heard, of the punishments meted out because of the conspiracy.

"Were a lot of people killed, Uncle?"

"Indeed, Nephew, a great many of those who are now called Huguenots. I saw them as they walked to the scaffold. I heard them sing as they were led to the axeman. 'God be merciful to us and bless us,' that's what they sang. As the heads of these men were struck off, one by one, the psalm singing grew fainter and fainter. Even the last man kept on singing until it was his turn to die. The axe grew blunted—"

He stopped as Jeanne came into the great hall.

"Henri, you should be with Monsieur Cayet. He is looking for you."

Uncle Condé smiled at Henri.

"We'll talk more later. We can go for a ride in the country. But your mother is right. You must not neglect your studies."

After the boy left, Jeanne sat down and asked her brother-in-law a question which had bothered her since his arrival the previous night.

"What are you going to do if François summons you back?"

Jeanne drummed her fingers nervously on the edge of her chair as she spoke. She knew as well as Condé did that Antoine was also implicated in the plot. Condé shrugged.

"We will cross that bridge when we come to it. Meanwhile I thank you for your hospitality."

In spite of the Amboise Conspiracy, the summer of 1560 was a good summer in Navarre. Nérac and the surrounding countryside bustled with activity. The Huguenot religion was preached openly. Streets resounded to the chanting of psalms. Religious pamphlets were sold freely in bookshops as well as in the marketplace. There was an air of contentment and happiness in the country, and young Henri ran about barefoot, cheerfully taking it all in.

"We shall get a visitor tomorrow, Henri."

Jeanne spoke to her son as they were out in the countryside, riding side by side through the hills and valleys of Béarn. They often did this, and it pleased the people to see them together, for they loved their queen and her son more than they did Antoine. Béarn countryside in the summer was robed in wildflowers. Reddish ferns grew on the slopes while on the crests of the mountains, rough rock outcroppings appeared like great, jagged scars. Below the mountains green pastures appeared startlingly soft against the rugged outline of the Pyrenees.

"I know," Henri answered his mother, "that Monsieur Théodore de Bèze shall come, and that he has traveled all the way from Geneva in Switzerland."

"Yes, and he shall teach us many things."

"Of what religion are we, Mother?"

Startled, Jeanne looked at her son. Why should he ask such a thing? Were not all their services conducted in the new faith?

Henri ducked a low-lying branch, bade his mother be careful, and rambled on.

"Monsieur Cayet, he says that you are Catholic, and I said, 'No, my mother is not Catholic.' But he says you have never publicly said that you are not a Catholic."

He stopped. A small waterfall cascaded down from a crag above them on their right. On their left, a few feet below them in a patch of open terrain, a green woodpecker hopped about looking for ants. At first the bird did not seem to mind the horses on the trail above him, but suddenly, as if the noise was finally too much, he took to the air. Flying away from them in a rising and falling motion, it cried. It was a pleasant, laughing sort of noise and took Jeanne back to when she had gone for rides with Monsieur Perault.

"It's going to rain," she said.

Henri laughed.

"How do you know?" he said.

Happy with the diversion, she told him many of the things Monsieur Perault had taught her when she was a young girl. Henri forgot what he had asked her, at least for that moment.

If small Henri had been boyishly frank with his question, Monsieur de Bèze was just as direct. But his directness was aimed at Antoine.

"Why, Your Majesty, do you not openly support the Huguenot cause? Many people look to you to lead them. God has placed you in a position of authority."

Antoine shrugged. He had no quarrel with being a member of the Huguenot faith when he was here, in Nérac, but if he went back to Paris, well, then if it served his purposes, he embraced the Catholic faith. But he was not about to tell his straight-laced guest such a thing. He smiled at Monsieur de Bèze. The fellow was a most excellent preacher, but he would not leave well enough alone.

"I will think about it."

"You must do more than think."

But Monsieur de Bèze spoke to the wall. Antoine had gotten up and left him alone.

"There is a letter from the king of France for you, Antoine."

Jeanne had the message in her hands and was visibly agitated. She had been dreading the day when François would summon Antoine.

Mon Oncle,

You doubtless will remember what I wrote you concerning the plot at Amboise. You will recall that many prisoners accused your brother, the Prince of Condé, of being involved. I have decided to investigate the matter myself. I charge you, therefore, to bring your brother to Orléans. If he will not come, I trust that you, mon Oncle Antoine, will make it clear to him that he must obey his king.

"Do not go, Antoine."

"It is a command, Jeanne, a command from the king."

"The king is a boy, Antoine, and he is commanded by his wife's uncles. You and Condé will walk into a trap."

"You are probably right."

Antoine sat down, undecided and nervous. But a few moments later he stood up again.

"I think I must go. I am, after all, a Prince of the Blood. They would not dare to harm me or Condé."

Condé agreed with Antoine, and nothing Jeanne said could make them change their minds.

28

BETRAYAL AND DEATH

About a week and a half after their departure Jeanne received a letter from Antoine.

My dear wife,

After a long journey through country torn with strife, we arrived at Orléans. The city square was barricaded and flanked with soldiers and the palace itself had a double guard. As we crossed the courtyard, there was little respect shown to us who are Princes of the Blood. From the courtyard we entered the audience room and only I was allowed to go in to see the king. He was with his mother and the Guise brothers.

François seemed too frail to stand erect. His eyes, as he looked at me, watered constantly and he was so pale that I believe him not long for this world. I bowed but François barely acknowledged it, although he indicated I should also bow to his mother. There was no warmth in him at all and I greatly regretted believing that Condé and I should have safe conduct.

When I spoke of clearing Condé's name, the only answer I received was to be present at his arrest. Jeanne, my dear wife, my brother is now in the prison of Amboise. Eléonore has begged the queen mother for his life but to no avail. He is to be tried for treason and I believe those who are trying him have already condemned him in their hearts.

As for me, I am not much better than a prisoner . . .

Jeanne read and reread the letter with much consternation, although in her heart she was not surprised. She wasted no time. Gathering Henri, baby Catherine, and her household about her, she informed them they would immediately move to the fortress of Navarreux.

Built in medieval times by Sancho of Navarre, Navarreux was located on the western frontier of Béarn. Jeanne's father had rebuilt it with thick walls and angled bastions. It was able to withstand cannon fire and had protected platforms for artillery, positioned in such a way as to give defenders a great range of fire. As she entered the grim but solid castle, Jeanne remembered going to Plessis as a child. She vividly recalled the bars in front of the windows and glanced at Henri as he happily and companionably rode his horse next to her . . . as she would have ridden to Plessis if her mother had been at her side. The horses' hooves echoed as they cantered over the moat.

Henri was a source of joy to Jeanne. She watched with pride as he studied with Monsieur Cayet who had nothing but good to say about the boy. He could recite Latin and Greek with ease and enjoyed reading. He rode horses skillfully and demonstrated great mastery at swordplay. But he was also tenderly affectionate with his baby sister Catherine and could suddenly turn to his mother, put his arm about her waist and hug her, even when there were servants close by.

They had been at Navarreux only a few weeks when a messenger from Orléans came to Jeanne with another letter from Antoine. It was December now and bitterly cold. Jeanne, Henri, Cayet, and several ladies were seated in the great hall in front of a roaring fire. Baby Catherine played, with a nurse watching her, on a blanket by the hearth. Jeanne took the letter in hand, opened the seal, and read silently to herself. Henri, unable to restrain himself, got up from where he was lounging on the floor by his sister, and read over her shoulder. Jeanne was already into the second page.

After Condé's imprisonment, Madame Catherine, the Queen Mother, summoned me to her apartments. She was concerned about François who was ill. It first seemed as if he suffered from a normal earache, something he has been prone to from childhood on. But then it was reported that there was a lump behind his ear the size of a walnut and that his ear was discharging a black and pussy substance. He was weak and often unable to speak. Madame Catherine was most friendly and had most excellent manners in this interview. She put her arm through mine and called me "dear brother of Navarre."

Jeanne sniffed angrily and put the letter down in her lap for an instant. She could see Madame Catherine's broad face, her pale fish-like eyes, her large nose, and her thick lower lip. "Most friendly," Antoine said, and "most excellent manners." Well, she did not trust the queen mother as far as she could throw her. Henri, at her back, laughed out loud, a sound which made his sister crow in delight. He ran over to her and tickled her tummy before he came back to his mother's chair.

"Father liked that very well, I wager. Having the queen mother call him brother."

Jeanne made no answer but only sighed as she picked up the letter again.

Madame Catherine went on to reassure me that she was very sorry for poor Condé's imprisonment and that she would do all in her power to help us. The physician, she then said, was quite sure François would not live. She wept here and I had to console her and do you remember, my Jeanne, how very sad it is to lose a child?

Jeanne put the letter down again. Of course she remembered. But she doubted the queen mother's grief. She had often seen how Madame Catherine had ignored and ill-treated her children when they were small. No, it was very likely, she was merely pretending to weep.

"Read on, ma mère," Henri prodded.

She turned back to the letter.

The queen mother confided in me that if François died, her son Charles would be the next king of France. He is quite young, only nine, you recall. We quite agreed that a boy of such a tender age cannot rule, especially when the country is split by religious warfare.

To Henri's chagrin, Jeanne put the letter down again.

"A regency," she said, "there will be a regency. And your father, as First Prince of the Blood, will assume power. This is tradition, and he shall have to establish a council to govern with him. A good council! With perhaps Monsieur Coligny, an honest man, who is now of the Reformed faith. God willing, upon François's death, your father shall rule France and he shall be able to put an end to the bloodshed going on in all the provinces right now. What a blessing!"

She smiled at Henri and at her ladies and waved at little Catherine who was cooing at the flames in the hearth.

"Read on then, mother! Read on!" Henri danced in excitement behind her chair.

She retrieved the letter, which had slid down her dress to the floor.

Even though regency is a possibility, Madame Catherine pointed out to me quite rightly, that Condé is still in prison and I myself am under close watch. As such, she advised that I would be wise to forfeit the regency to herself. She then proposed to undertake the role of protectress for both Condé and myself and because of her high personal regard for me, to appoint me Lieutenant General of France when the time should come, God forbid, that François should die.

Jeanne crumpled the letter with her right hand and spoke softly but distinctly as if to herself.

"Out of fear and for a fancy title he gives up a God-given task!"

She eyed the messenger who had ridden posthaste with the news and who was discreetly warming himself by the hearth.

"Have you further news?"

He bowed low before he answered her.

"Yes, Your Majesty. King François died the night of December 5."

29

CONFESSION OF FAITH

There was no need really, to stay on at the fortress of Navarreux. Jeanne soon received word that Condé had been released and that the Guise brothers no longer held any power. Madame Catherine de Medicis, as Queen Mother, now stood at the head of France. Antoine occupied a position of favor. She bristled at the phrase "a position of favor." It sounded rather like a dog being petted. Shame filled her as she packed. Another letter from Antoine was in her pocket urging her to come to court.

Jeanne felt strongly that the French court was no place for herself and the children. Catherine Medicis coveted power and would like nothing better than to get her fingers on Navarre. Jeanne, therefore, wrote Antoine back to say that she would stay home, in Navarre, and she urged him to come back as well.

Regardless of the chill, December temperature, people came out of their homes to cheer her and to wave her on as she rode back to Pau. She waved back, her mind partly clearing from the grief she felt at Antoine's foolishness. At one point, because of bad weather, they were forced to stop for a few hours at a local *jauregiak*, or manor house. So much love and hospitality was shown that Jeanne's spirits lifted.

Bowing, the host escorted her and her ladies into his simple whitewashed dwelling. She walked into the *eskaratza* of his home, past the housing carts, into the *sala*, the huge parlor, which she knew was only used for special occasions.

"Would Your Majesty care for some food?"

She accepted graciously and watched with happiness as her son ambled into the kitchen to speak with the servants. She rose and followed him and remembered that Henri had grown up in one of these estates. Hams, onions, and scarlet peppers were suspended from the low rafters. A wooden bench stood close to the fire, and a walnut dresser displayed some crockery. Shelves built into the wall held pots and pans, and some children played on the floor. Deep within herself Jeanne envied the people who lived here.

"Can you read?"

She addressed her host, a short, stocky man named Jacques Martel. His shirt was clean, and his brown doublet and jerkin smelled of wood smoke. He nodded.

"And what do you read?" Jeanne continued, intrigued.

"I have," he answered, "a Bible, Marot's Psalms, and also an almanac."

The children at the hearth sang softly.

Celebrate without ceasing
the goodness of God*

*Célébrons sans cesse; de Dieu les bontés.

It was a round, and Henri, ever the cheerful musician, sat by them and joined in singing.

"Your wife," said Jeanne, looking around and noting only the servants, "I have not met your good wife."

"She died in the autumn of last year. She had a swelling in her breast and became ill. There was nothing to be done."

He stopped and looked at the floor.

"I'm sorry."

He smiled at her.

"You know death yourself, Your Majesty. Haven't you buried some of your babes?"

He stopped, a little shocked at his own familiarity.

"It's all right, Monsieur Martel."

Jeanne had seen compassion in his eyes and did not mind. He continued.

"It's only bearable because God upholds, isn't that so, Your Majesty?"

She nodded, tears in her eyes, but her heart felt strangely stirred.

"It will be Christmas soon, Maman."

Henri had come to her side as she spoke to Monsieur Martel. He whispered the words with suppressed excitement.

She smiled and said, "Yes, it will."

"We shall be home in Pau, and Monsieur Boisnormand or Monsieur David will preach, and we shall have a special meal and games. Yes?"

She nodded and then sighed.

"Do you miss Father?"

"Yes, I do."

"But I am here, Maman."

He suddenly broke into the Basque language.

"*Nire aitaren etxea defendituko dut*, I shall defend the house of my father."

Henri's curly brown hair framed a serious, although often mischievous, face. He placed his firm hand in hers.

She stroked his cheek and answered, "There is no need, Son. We have a Defender. You know this. Monsieur Cayet teaches you this as well as Monsieur Boisnormand."

"But I shall fight—"

"Hush!" Jeanne said. "Hush, my son!"

They arrived in Pau two days before Christmas. Jeanne asked Monsieur Boisnormand to prepare to have the Lord's Supper served on Christmas morning in the castle's chapel. She herself spent much time there in prayer. Antoine had not sent any more letters. It sat like a lump in her chest that, except for his inability to see beyond his own foolishness, the Huguenot religion might have become the religion of France.

"Maman, Catherine is crying."

Henri appeared at the chapel door, agitated and red in the face.

"Why, is she ill?"

"I think she fell down," the boy replied.

Jeanne rose in haste, remembering another child who had fallen and she had not been told. She ran with Henri to the nursery. Catherine, in the arms of Suzanne de Bourbon, a distant cousin, was quiet but upon seeing her mother, began wailing loudly.

"What is—" Jeanne began, but Suzanne gestured that everything was all right.

"She tumbled off her chair and scraped her knee, but she is fine."

Jeanne took the child and sat down, rocking her back and forth. How she loved her two children, and how she thanked God for them. Catherine put her fingers into her mouth. She was teething and drooled horribly. Henri pranced around reciting,

> Pick not thy teeth at the table sitting,
> Nor use at thy meat over much spitting;
> This rudeness of youth is to be abhorred;
> Thyself mannerly behave at the board.

Suzanne swatted at him. "Do not make fun of Master Seager's rules for good manners, young master. Catherine is only a baby, and it took you long enough to learn manners, if indeed you do know them."

Henri laughed and continued dancing around. "Don't you feel good, Mother? And tomorrow is Christmas."

She laughed with him, hugging the small body of Catherine to her own.

"Yes, indeed, I do, Henri."

Christmas Day in Pau during that winter of 1560 dawned clear and bright. Jeanne awoke early. She lay quietly on her side of the great bed and wondered if Antoine would ever come back to share it with her again. Reaching out for his pillow, she fingered its edge. The softness of it caressed her, and she remembered very clearly how he had wept when she had told him of their first child. That was a long time ago.

Would he weep with love at anything she told him now? She swallowed and blinked back tears.

"Be of good courage."

Those were the words Monsieur David had used when he preached last night. Afterward she had spoken to him about the sermon. She tried to remember all he had said.

"You must love the Lord, and trust him, Your Majesty."

Antoine was gone right now. Her parents were also gone, mere shadows and insubstantial.

"I am alone, Monsieur David. My husband, well, I do not think that he will ever fully renounce the papist religion."

"God will be pleased to give you courage, Madame, if you trust Him. He can and will, by His grace, make you strong so that even the most threatening power cannot move you," the minister assured her. "Those who obey God may be sure of His favor. That is to say, if you are not ashamed of Him here in Navarre, He will make you a rock able to withstand anything."

She had not answered. Monsieur Martel, when she had spoken to him of the wealth of his home, had exclaimed, "What are my riches! The Lord is my friend!"

All these conversations tumbled about in her head. Her Bible lay on the chest directly opposite the bed. She longed to hold it and read some of the passages Monsieur David had explained. But it was chilly—Yvette had not yet come to light the hearth. On an impulse she whipped back the down covers and jumped out of bed. Her bare feet rebelled against the icy coldness of the floor, and she squealed like a young girl as she ran across the room to grab the Bible. Racing back into bed, she pulled the covers over both her and the Bible. Curling up like a baby, she waited until she was warm again. There was a sweet comfort, to lie thus with God's Word against her.

Later that morning, as Jeanne's household gathered together to celebrate the wonderful communion of the Lord's Supper in the chapel, she remained comforted. Indeed, a strength beyond her own carried her to the front of the church after the service. Monsieur David motioned that everyone should be seated, that Madame the Queen wished to speak to them. Jeanne had dressed simply. Her red velvet gown was not ornate, and her brown hair was drawn back by a simple, black headdress. A single string of pearls hung about her neck, and, as she gazed at the people seated before her in the pews, her face was gentle and smiling.

"Dear people," she said and then stopped, emotion threatening to overcome her even as she began.

She felt more acutely than ever that Antoine should be at her side. But even as she trembled in her aloneness, she felt another Presence and was able to continue.

"The times are such that it appears necessary for people of good standing to come out openly and declare what they believe. I wish you all to know, and declare to you publicly, that on this day in which we celebrate the birth of our Lord and Savior, I here take a stand for the Huguenot faith."

A ripple of excitement passed through the church. Jeanne looked at the faces turned up to her and saw beyond them. It seemed as if they suddenly were, together with herself and her children, part of a great multitude—one she could not number.

"As such," Jeanne continued, "I declare that Navarre and all the surrounding territories which are under my domain, shall henceforth be ruled accordingly by the grace of God."

There was a intense silence. Jeanne swallowed and went on.

"I say this and will act on it at the risk of my crown, my wealth, and my children."

A load fell off her shoulders—she felt as if she had wings. She saw with clarity where the great multitude was going. For was she not walking with them now? In the distance stood Someone with a crown, brighter than her own; Someone with a scepter greater than her own; and Someone who opened his arms to her and called her his child.

EPILOGUE

After Jeanne d'Albret's open profession of faith on Christmas Day 1560, she consistently led a life of faithfulness to God. Her remaining time was only twelve years, but she used those years well.

After her declaration, nine-year-old Henri, the future Henri IV of France, was almost immediately taken from her by Antoine, who publicly avowed his allegiance to Roman Catholicism. The queen mother tried to convince Jeanne of the wisdom of converting back to the Roman Catholic faith in order to regain both her husband, who threatened divorce, and her son. But Jeanne said, "If I held my kingdom and my son in my hand, I would rather throw both into the bottom of the sea than to attend Mass."

In 1562 the Wars of Religion began to sweep through France in earnest. Protestants and Catholics began to fight one another in a series of devastating wars that would last thirty-six years with periods of truce in between. Within a year of the onset of these wars, Antoine was killed. (If he had made himself head of the Huguenots, Calvinism might have become the religion of France.) Jeanne, as sole ruler of the domain in the southwest, made Calvinism the state religion of Béarn. Henri, who became First Prince of the Blood upon the death of his father, was held as a hostage at the French court until 1567. At this time Jeanne was finally allowed to take him home to Béarn.

When the pope threatened Jeanne because of her Protestant stand, she responded:

> I condemn no one to death or to imprisonment. I blush for you and feel ashamed when you falsely state that many atrocities have been done by those of our religion. You allege authority over many countries. I acknowledge over me in Béarn God only, to whom I shall render account of the people He has committed to my care. As in no point I have deviated from the faith of God's Holy Catholic Church, I bid you keep your tears to deplore your own errors that you may be restored to the true fold, and become a faithful shepherd instead of a hireling. I desire that your useless letter may be the last of its kind.

Jeanne passed laws to protect the ministers who faithfully preached the gospel in her kingdom. She abolished public processions and took the images out of churches. Where the majority of inhabitants in her cities were Protestant, the cathedrals were given to them for their use; where the inhabitants were equally divided, the two faiths shared the church buildings. Monasteries were converted to schools; colleges were founded for higher education; the Bible was translated into Basque dialects; and ministers from Geneva continued to preach the gospel.

All these things Jeanne did at the risk of her life. During the twelve years she ruled as a Protestant sovereign, she was singled out as the enemy of the papacy, the nobles of France,

Philip of Spain, and others. They called her rude names such as "Jezebel," "mad slut," and "the furious she-beast."

During her reign, Béarn and the surrounding districts flourished. Good husbandry, encouragement of arts, and fair law all formed a huge contrast to the disorder, violence, and poverty in other countries. No beggar was seen by the wayside, and no child was permitted to grow up without an education.

In 1572, Catherine de Médicis proposed a marriage between her daughter, Marguerite of Valois, and Henri of Navarre. Jeanne was not in favor, but other Huguenot leaders persuaded her that the marriage might prove to be the end of hostilities between the Huguenots and the Catholics. Jeanne traveled to Paris to arrange the wedding with Catherine, and, while there, she fell ill and died. Many people believe she was poisoned by Catherine de Médicis.

Henri of Navarre did marry Marguerite. But the wedding was a trap, which had been arranged to entice Huguenots to Paris, culminating in the infamous St. Bartholomew's Day Massacre. Henri of Navarre himself survived the massacre by converting to Catholicism. Like his father, he often wavered in areas of faith and over the years fluctuated between one religion and the other.

Henri, through the providence of God, proclaimed the Edict of Nantes in 1598—a law that established religious toleration for almost one hundred years. By this edict Huguenots were given freedom of worship, freedom to hold public office, freedom of education, and certain fortified towns. A prosperous time began. Schools and churches flourished, and people became "as the wings of a dove covered with silver" (Psalm 68:13).

The Edict of Nantes was overturned in 1685, and the French Huguenots once again became a persecuted and martyred church. Thousands of people were driven into exile. God weaves strange patterns into history, scattering his seed among the tares and shaking his salt into the cauldron of nations. So it was that these exiles, bereft of country but not of Truth, fled to places such as England, Holland, Prussia, and America. There they settled, integrated with other cultures, and spoke Truth. Today we cannot put our finger on a specific geographical area—whether township or county—where we might find the Huguenots. But we see them seeking the shadow of the Almighty in the annals of history. They and their great leader Jeanne d'Albret inspire us to rise on the wings of faith.

Author's Note

Wings Like a Dove is a fictionalized portrait of Jeanne d'Albret. Much of it is drawn from the sources listed in the bibliography. I have tried to be as factual as possible with dates, events, and names. However, a number of times I invented, or imagined, if you will, how Jeanne would have done or said something. For example, Jeanne did in fact cut out a fox's face from a tapestry and inserted a monk's face instead. The "when" and "how" of this event, however, I made up. Most of the people mentioned in the story actually existed. But Yvette, Jeanne's personal maid, is fictional and serves only as a way of conveying the spirit and nature of the household and times.

My prayer is that the remarkable odyssey of Jeanne d'Albret will reassure readers that God is completely in control of their lives, and that this book will challenge them to work out their salvation with a joyful and submissive spirit.

GLOSSARY

Albret: Royal family of Navarre. Henri d'Albret was more than just the king of Navarre. He was also the Viscount of Béarn, Bigorre, Gabarolan, Marsan, and Nébouzan, as well as Duke of Armagnac and Count of Fézenzaguet, Foix, Limousin, and Périgord. All this made him, as it were, viceroy over the whole French region of Aquitaine, also known as Guyenne.

bailli: A ranking officer in the royal administration of the provinces of France. **Baillive** is the feminine equivalent of bailli.

Bastille: A fortress in Paris built in the 14ᵗʰ century and used as a prison.

Battle of Pavia: A 1525 battle in Italy in which the French army was utterly defeated by Spain and in which Emperor Charles V took Francis I prisoner. He was later freed on several conditions: that he marry the Emperor's sister, Eleanor, and that his two oldest sons be held in Spain as hostages. (After several years the princes were returned to France.) In this battle France also lost Burgundy, as well as right over Flanders, Artois, Genoa, Milan, and Naples.

Béarn: Navarre's neighbor and an independent sovereignty. Its viscount, Jeanne's father, governed through Béarn's Estates made up of an equal number of clergy, nobles, and commoners. The Estates had the right to be consulted on all important affairs. Through Jeanne's father, they objected to her marriage to the Duke of Clèves.

Berquin: A nobleman and one of King Francis I's councillors. He was imprisoned in 1525 for favoring Reformed teachings and rescued by Princess Marguerite's intervention. In 1528, when the king was away from Paris, he was rearrested, quickly condemned, and burned at the stake.

biggens: Caps.

caltrop: An iron ball with four projecting spikes so disposed that when the ball was on the ground one of them always pointed upwards. Caltrops were used to obstruct the passage of cavalry. Louis XI, who had built Plessis, had scattered caltrops randomly throughout surrounding lanes so that no one could approach the château deviously.

caparison: Decorative covering for a horse.

clock: A short embroidered ornament on the outer side of a stocking from the ankle upward.

Conspiracy of Amboise: An ambush carried out at the château of Amboise where the teenage King François often stayed with his court. Led by a Calvinist, Sieur de la Renaudie, its intent was to spirit the young king away from his wicked uncles, to present a petition of grievances to François, and to arrest the Guise brothers.

Council of Trent: A Council called by the Roman Catholic Church which met for a number of years at different times during the 1540s and 50s to discuss questions such as "Can someone be saved by faith and works?" and "How many sacraments are there?"

d'Ètaples, Jacques Lefèvre: A Bible scholar (1455-1536) who taught that man was saved, not by works, but by God's mercy and grace. Charged with heresy and forced to flee for his life, he went to Nérac where he died peacefully, nursed by Marguerite. Calvin was much influenced by his teaching.

eskaratza: Vast hall.

genuflect: To bend the knee in worship.

hostelry: Inn.

Huguenots: After the Conspiracy of Amboise this name was given to those of the Reformed faith. The origin of the word is uncertain. The most plausible source of the name, and there are many, is from the word *Eidgenossen* , or "those who together keep faith." It was a term that came from Geneva.

jauregiak: Manor house.

kirtle: A loose gown or skirt which could be worn underneath an outer garment.

La Flèche: A château at which Aymée cared for little Prince Henri, the small Duke of Beaumont.

livre tournois: A French gold coin.

Mardi Gras: The day before Lent, celebrated in Paris as a day of merrymaking.

Mercuriale: A meeting by the representatives of all the principal courts of France to investigate and admonish each other to vigilance for the country. Francis I had ordered these meetings to be held every three months on a Wednesday—Dies Mercurii—hence they were named Mercuriales.

Navarre: Small country between France and Spain. Its importance lay in the Pyrenees which ran smack through its middle. Whoever held these high mountain passes could make either French invasion of Spain possible or Spanish invasion of France possible.

Marot: (c. 1497-1544) a French poet and hymnist. A resident of Francis I's court, he attacked the abuses of the Roman Catholic Church and was imprisoned. When released, he favored Reformed teaching and translated the Psalms into poetic meter. Many of these were used by Calvin in a psalter.

Papacy: System of Roman Catholic church government in which the pope is recognized as the supreme and infallible head. A papist is, therefore, one who gives allegiance to the papacy.

Prince (or Princess) of the Blood: One who, by virtue of parentage, was heir (or heiress) to the throne of France after a reigning king's legitimate male successor.

rails: Nightdresses.

rushes: Dried grass, herbs, and plants used as a floor covering to hide dirt and to keep rooms sweet-smelling.

sweetmeat: Delicacy or candy prepared with sugar.

stitchet: Corset.

tchirula: A long, narrow drum.

ttun-ttun: Tambourine.

Waldensians: In the last years of François I's life, persecution against the Reformers increased. A large massacre took place in certain villages along the Durance in 1545. Twenty-four people were burned, and over 800 people were slaughtered. The people who lived and worshiped here were known as the Waldensians. Their only crime was that they read the Bible and rejected the mass, the pope, and purgatory.

BIBLIOGRAPHY

Ardagh, John. *Writers' France*. London: Hamish Hamilton, 1989.

Baird, Henry M. *History of the Rise of the Huguenots in France*. 2 vols. New York: Charles Scribner's Sons, 1895.

Bryson, David. *Queen Jeanne and the Promised Land*. Leiden: Brill, 1999.

Caro, Ina. *The Road From the Past*. New York: Doubleday, 1994.

Cormier, Anne Denieul. *A Time of Glory*. Garden City, NY: Doubleday, 1968.

Davidson, Marshall B. *The Horizon Concise History of France*. New York: American Heritage, 1971.

De Boulay, F. R. H. *An Age of Ambition*. New York: Viking Press, 1970.

De Plessis, Mlle. Translated by Lucy Crump. *A Huguenot Family in the XVI Century*. New York: George Routledge and Sons, 1824.

Gray, Janet Glenn. *The French Huguenots*. Grand Rapids: Baker, 1981.

Hackett, Francis. *Francis the First*. Garden City, NY: Doubleday, 1935.

Hopkins, Lisa. *Women Who Would Be Kings*. London: Vision Press, 1991.

"Huguenots and the Wars of Religion." *Christian History*, 20:71 no. 3, entire issue.

Kurlansky, Mark. *The Basque History of the World*. Canada: Vintage, 1999.

Law, Joy. *Fleur de Lys: The Kings and Queens of France*. London: Hamish Hamilton, 1976.

Pardoe, Julia. *The Court and Reign of Francis the First, King of France,* vols. 2, 3. London: Richard Bentley and Son, 1887.

Putnam, Samuel. *Marguerite of Navarre.* New York: Grosset and Dunlop, 1935.

Roelker, Nancy Lyman. *Queen of Navarre: Jeanne d'Albret.* Cambridge, MA: Belnap Press of Harvard University Press, 1968.

Sanger, Andrew. *Exploring Rural France.* 3rd. ed. Lincolnwood, IL: Passport Books, 1993.

Strage, Mark. *Women of Power.* New York and London: Harcourt Brace Jovanovich, 1976.

Sturrock, John. *The French Pyrenees.* London: Faber and Faber, 1988.

Wylie, J. A. *The History of Protestantism.* Kilkeel, N. Ireland: Mourne Missionary Trust, 1878.

Christine Farenhorst, author and poet, is a columnist for *Reformed Perspective*, a contributing writer for *Christian Renewal*, and a reviewer for Christian Schools International. She is the author of *Amazing Stories from Times Past, The Great Escape, Suffer Annie Spence, The Letter Child*, and *Before My Mother's Womb*. Farenhorst has also written a collection of poems and co-authored two church history textbooks for children. She and her husband, Anco, have five children, seventeen grandchildren, a dog, and ten chickens.